00661582

BOARDROOM EXCELLENCE

A Common Sense Perspective on Corporate Governance

Paul P. Brountas

Copyright © 2003 Paul P. Brountas
Published by Hale and Dorr LLP

All rights reserved. No part of this publication may be reproduced or transmitted in any form or by any means, electronic or mechanical, including photocopy, recording or any information storage or retrieval system, without permission in writing from the author or publisher.

The materials and recommendations contained in this book are based on the author's experience. Nothing contained in this publication is to be considered as the rendering of legal advice for specific cases, and readers are responsible for obtaining such advice from their own legal counsel.

Printed in the United States of America

COVER ILLUSTRATION BY ROY SCOTT

PHOTOGRAPH OF PAUL P. BROUNTAS BY BILL O'CONNELL

For

LYNN

My Moral Compass

Preface

Paul Brountas has written a superlative analysis of the crisis in corporate governance that in the last several years has undermined the integrity of our markets, proved devastating to millions of investors and workers, and sapped the strength of our economy. Having served as outside counsel to hundreds of corporations over the course of his long and distinguished legal career, and in that capacity having attended literally thousands of corporate board and executive committee meetings, the author speaks with real knowledge and authority.

The appeal of this "extended essay" will reach a readership far beyond the limits of the boardroom. Paul Brountas' uncommon experience is fully matched by his uncommon wisdom and a large and welcome measure of solid common sense. *Boardroom Excellence: A Common Sense Perspective on Corporate Governance* reflects all three. It explains clearly and succinctly what went wrong in the boardrooms of too many of our publicly owned companies and sets out reform measures to ensure that these abuses will not happen again. Written in a forthright and accessible style that avoids the pitfalls of formal legal prose, it will prove invaluable to everyone concerned about the future of corporate governance and the fairness and transparency of our markets.

This important contribution to the literature on corporate governance is especially timely. Over the past two years, successive waves of corporate failures have focused national attention on pervasive problems with accounting, auditing, and corporate governance practices. We are now dealing with the consequences of those abuses: trillions of dollars in market value gone, investors' savings lost and their confidence undermined, workers unemployed, the global reputation of our markets badly tarnished.

In the public sector, a broad effort is under way to deal with abuses in accounting, auditing, and corporate governance procedures and market practices. With landmark legislation enacted last summer, the Congress created the statutory framework for reform, eliminating numerous practices that led to egregious conflicts of interest and assuring to the Securities and Exchange Commission the broader authority, staff resources, and advanced technology it must have to carry out effectively the broad range of its regulatory responsibilities. Implementation of the legislation is proceeding on schedule; the SEC has now put in place the new Public Accounting Oversight Board, thereby ending the system of self-regulation in that industry which had failed so disastrously to ensure the independence of public company auditors.

Statutory and regulatory measures are absolutely essential to effective reform, but corresponding efforts must also be undertaken in the private sector. The self-regulatory agencies, the National Association of Securities Dealers and the New York Stock Exchange, have begun a critical analysis of corporate governance and conflicts of interest, and are moving toward more stringent listing standards.

In addition, there is an urgent need for greater public understanding of just what caused the crisis in corporate governance, of the reforms that corporate management and directors must now adopt, and of the expanding opportunities for shareholders to make their voices heard in the boardroom. *Boardroom Excellence: A Common Sense Perspective on Corporate Governance* provides a penetrating analysis and a clear prescription for the future. It therefore deserves the widest possible readership. While every CEO, director, and prospective director of a public company should find it indispensable, its utility is not limited to corporate executives and boards; it is written for everyone concerned about our capital markets. Paul Brountas has done a first-rate job of explaining what went wrong—and what is needed to set things right. This book could not have come at a better time.

—Senator Paul S. Sarbanes
May 2003

Foreword

The demise of Enron and the attendant revelations have spawned a body of "literature" almost as capacious as the scandal itself. Much of what has been written was obviously written in haste, some was just an exercise in self-righteousness, and almost all arrived in a prose style long ago dismissed by Kenneth Galbraith as "free enterprise Simple Simon." Worse still, there was remarkably little by way of common sensical advice for people who actually sat in boardrooms. Pundits, in their zeal to tell directors how evil and indolent they were, didn't pause to tell them how they might do a better job.

Boardroom Excellence: A Common Sense Perspective on Corporate Governance remedies that lack and perhaps, more astonishingly, proves that some lawyers can actually write. Paul Brountas comes from Maine, and its terse and understated qualities are his. His mission is simple: to take 40 years of advising officers and directors, and distill it into 84 pages without producing either a self-help book or a paean to those who made a bundle and lived to tell about it. Here at last is the true adult voice of a lawyer reminding us what matters is not theory but experience.

That experience, Paul's experience, is now available for all of us to draw on. He explains there never was an Edenic past in which all right-thinking folk admired Corporate America. He shows how persons of good will gradually slipped from grace, lost their moorings, and let the deviant become the norm. He offers the archetypes of the bad board members — "the sleeper," "the rapper," "the know-it-all"—and provides the most comprehensive guide to the best boardroom practices anyone could wish for.

The book and movie reviewing industries have, for all time, destroyed the value of high praise, no matter how honestly tendered. Even the worst flick will find a critic in suburban Duluth to hail it as "the best damn movie I've seen in years." So, no such plaudits here, only a restrained plea that those who manage corporations, serve on their boards, or aspire either to manage or to serve take an afternoon off, read what Paul has written, and reflect on the lessons he offers. It will do them—and the country—incalculable good.

—JEFFREY RUDMAN
Chair, Corporate and Securities Litigation Group
Hale and Dorr LLP
May 2003

CONTENTS

"My bleak historical portrayal of Corporate America is not
intended as a blanket condemnation of all publicly traded corporations." • The Good Old Days • The Great Bubble • Making
the Numbers by "Making Up" the Numbers • Wealth Creation
and Corporate Hero Worship • Corporate America Lost Its
Moral Compass • The Sarbanes-Oxley Road Map

"It is the right, and obligation, of every director to be informed
and to act deliberately, with the diligence and competence of a
reasonably prudent person in a similar situation under like circumstances." • Business Judgment Rule • Loss of Reputation
and Embarrassment

"Excellent companies stay excellent by regularly challenging
themselves." • Why Serve as a Director? • CEO-Dominated
Process • What Should Directors Do? .

"The board has no room for insouciant directors who are not
committed or who believe they can serve by being passive
observers." • Disagreement Is a Virtue, Not a Vice

"The CEO should seek to create a board meeting environment
that encourages skepticism and serious discussion and enables
board members to disagree constructively." • Know Your Board
• Setting the Tone and Corporate Culture • The CEO's Role in
Decision-Making • What Keeps the CEO Awake at Night

Introduction

My experience as outside counsel to several hundred corporations and as an attendee at thousands of board and committee meetings over the past 42 years has taught me some important, often ignored, lessons about corporate governance:

- how recent widespread greed and dishonesty contaminated the corporate environment
- why corporate executives need committed, independent, and active oversight and assistance
- why corporate directors have failed to properly discharge their fiduciary duties and responsibilities
- why public cynicism has replaced public trust and confidence in our current form of corporate governance.

Many of these lessons are so obvious that they hardly warrant discussion. But something happened during the past several years, as the management and directors of so many U.S. corporations put their personal interests before the interests of stockholders. As a result, many public corporations in America are viewed today with distrust and disdain, a view brought about by executive avarice and a corrosive belief that opaqueness trumps transparency when it comes to public disclosure and that collegiality in the boardroom trumps independence when it comes to corporate governance.

How else can we explain:
- cooked books and phantom revenue
- Enron's special-purpose entities whose undisclosed special purpose was to enrich insiders
- WorldCom's and Adelphia's massive executive loans
- Tyco's $20 million "tip" to a director and his favorite charity
- Global Crossing's round-trip "investments"
- skyrocketing executive compensation and Brobingnagian stock option awards
- enormous corporate debt that never made it to the balance sheet

- independent auditors who were so distracted by—if not obsessed with—the huge fees they earned from nonaudit work that they failed to appreciate that their independence might be compromised by their nonaudit services
- the expanding, corrosive culture of excess and hedonism
- the sordid recent history of millions of workers who have suffered painful pension plan losses
- the steady flow of new reports of dishonesty and ineptitude, "perp" walks, lawsuits, and public disgrace that have been so much a part of the opening years of the 21st century.

How Did It Happen—or Was It Always This Bad?

My bleak historical portrayal of

Corporate America is not intended

as a blanket condemnation of all

publicly traded U.S. corporations.

The "Good Old Days"

Time has a way of distorting memories—making the past look a lot better than it actually was, particularly when compared to current conditions. Those who believe that the egregious conduct and pernicious behavior of Enron and its ilk is a new phenomenon and yearn for the return of that golden era when corporations were compassionate, enlightened, and honest—and dedicated to serve the best interests of their stockholders—are either suffering from amnesia or delusion. The fact is that things were not so great in the "good old days."

The early 1900s saw the rise of the so-called "robber barons" and the immense power of a small group of corporate leaders, which led to the successful industrialization of America, followed by the 1929 stock market collapse, the painful Depression of the early 1930s, and the remedial legislative action by Congress in the enactment of the Securities Act of 1933 and the Securities Exchange Act of 1934.

The corporate world as we now know it, with thousands of publicly owned corporations operating globally, began to develop after World War II; grew at a steady rate over the next four decades; and flourished in the last decade of the 20th century as thousands of new, high-technology corporations were organized by brilliant, fearless scientists, engineers, and entrepreneurs and were financed by a seemingly endless supply of equity capital from venture capitalists, corporate sponsors, and public investors. As a result, at the start of the 21st century, America was home to thousands of publicly held corporations with millions of new public stockholders who owned equity in Corporate America individually or derivatively through participation in their mutual funds, pension funds, 401(k)s, and IRAs.

This new breed of stockholders relied on a system of corporate governance that had existed for decades, where, for many leading corporations, the center of gravity and power was the CEO. The board members were friends or business acquaintances of the CEO; the boardroom was expected to be collegial if not "clubby," with directors who neither desired nor were willing to rock the boat; and the checks and balances on board behavior were in large part governed by state corporate laws, particularly the Delaware Corporation Law which, while still friendly to corporate boards and management, has been amended over the years to promote board independence and protect and enhance the interests of the stockholders.

I need to pause here to reassure the reader that my bleak historical portrayal of Corporate America is not intended as a blanket condemnation of all publicly traded U.S. corporations. Most of the executives and directors I have had the privilege of advising are decent, ethical, responsible men and women whose paramount interest has been the enhancement of shareholder value and the creation of a corporate culture that rewards integrity and ethical behavior. They have demonstrated that they can be creative without being corrupt. They do their work quietly and effectively and, therefore, are rarely noted for their good work and successes publicly. However, what does receive public attention—and lots of it—are corporate scandals, greed, avarice, and fraud, all of which, and particularly those cases that involve hundreds of millions of dollars or instances of sybaritic behavior, lead the public to believe that the entire system is corrupt. On the other hand, corruption is contagious, and the more widespread it becomes, the more it infects and confuses those who want to do the right thing. Fortunately, there are notable examples of corporations that are governed by exemplary boards and operated by honest, shareholder-oriented executives. It is those corporations that we to look for guidance and that we seek to emulate.

The Great Bubble

The period of the Great Bubble, beginning in 1999 and ending in early 2001, witnessed a historic increase in the number of public corporations in America; unprecedented increases in the post-IPO stock prices of newly minted public corporations; growth of a new breed of investment analysts who publicly hyped the stock of their investment banking clients while privately denigrating those clients and their future prospects; a rapidly expanding group of multimillionaires (founders and executives of Internet and dot-com corporations in their mid- to late-twenties); a massive distribution of stock options to the corporation's executives and employees; and a new, widely accepted stock option program for nonemployee directors, designed to align the interests of directors with the corporation's stockholders. An intense focus on corporate stock ownership developed, and the daily trading price of stocks became the primary engine that drove and influenced the decisions of management and directors.

Stock options also had an effect on the business strategy of the corporation's board and management.. As the stock prices rose and the executives, employees, and directors saw the value of their options increase, both management and directors moved the corporation from the traditional long-term strategy to a strategy aimed at maximizing short-term performance. Each quarter's operating results determined whether the price would continue to rise. Corporate America became obsessed with quarterly performance and with the unrealistic expectation that each quarter's earnings would be higher than those of the previous quarter. Performance was measured not in dollars, but in pennies. Therefore, a one- or two-cent shortfall on the quarter's performance could wipe out millions of dollars of stockholder value. So management began to take—and encouraged their co-workers to take—whatever action was necessary to make sure that the quarterly results matched or exceeded the corporation's quarterly estimates.

Making the Numbers by "Making Up" the Numbers

It was not unusual for a CEO to call in the corporation's sales and marketing executives near the end of a quarter and deliver a compelling end-of-the-quarter warning, along the lines of:

"If we don't meet our quarterly earnings projections, our stock price will take a big hit, the value of your options will fall, your bonus will be in jeopardy, and you run the risk of not being awarded future stock options. So get out there; nail down the orders and sales that we need to make the quarter. I know you can find the additional revenue we need."

This form of challenge was treated by many in the audience to whom it was directed as "code" for: "Damn it, you know how to find the additional revenue that we need. Go get it, and I don't care how you get it." To negate that implicit call to create otherwise nonrecognizable revenue, the CEO should have said: "I know if you pull out all the stops, you can produce the additional revenue we need, but I don't want one additional cent of revenue that does not qualify as revenue under generally accepted accounting principles (GAAP)."

The failure to add the GAAP qualifier and the intense pressure to make the numbers led employees to "make up" the numbers and management to include them without ensuring that they were GAAP-proof.

This type of activity led to similar questionable activity, which skated close to the line of lawful behavior and in many cases crossed the line—questionable activity that management apparently had little incentive to question.

This started, in a manner similar to so many ethical meltdowns, with seemingly minor offenses. A salesman, for example, would tell his customer, "Here, take the shipment now, and if you can't resell it within the next three months, we'll take it back." The salesman would then proceed to include the shipment as revenue, even though the customer had a contractual right to return it.

This common failure to follow GAAP revenue-recognition policies as well as the growing tendency to look for loopholes led, over time, to even more creative fraudulent activities. These were hidden by the perpetrators and were not susceptible to board discovery because the directors had neglected to establish codes of conduct, ethical guidelines, monitoring programs, and a corporate culture that might have prevented the fraudulent acts or at least have helped—if properly administered—to establish a tone at the top and a culture throughout the organization that punished those who believed, "anything goes, but don't get caught."

Wealth Creation and Corporate Hero Worship

Each quarter's performance became the overriding concern, and when the forecast results were achieved, millions of people benefited from the increase in value of their investments. A feeling of empowerment, privilege, and even arrogance developed among the management types who were appearing on the covers of an ever-increasing number of financial publications as well as in flattering, worshipful articles in such stalwarts as *The Wall Street Journal* and *Time* magazine.

Who would be the next 28-year-old whiz kid to join the *Forbes* list of billionaires? Which of the new start-up technology corporations with a corporate history of less than two years would be acquired by Lucent or Cisco for more than a billion dollars of Lucent's or Cisco's then highly inflated stock?

Corporate America Lost Its Moral Compass

The laser beam focus on wealth creation and the unprecedented growth of individual paper wealth, coupled with the ease with which corporate valuations could be manipulated without detection, fed on itself and became, in the minds of many, the acceptable way to conduct business in America. It created and nourished a Zeitgeist of corporate hero worship, in which CEOs were treated like rock stars and ethical conduct and honesty were shunted aside, if not totally ignored. It was bound to collapse, because it was built on greed, hubris, and falsehoods. And just as it began to appear that it would never end, the whole Internet, dot-com house of cards collapsed. Stunned investors throughout America began to ask, "How did this happen?"

It happened because Corporate America lost its moral compass and there were no corporate cultural precedents on which it could rely. The leading American corporations of the first half of the 20th century, which were largely controlled by insiders (some of whom were even benevolent), did not serve as models for the future. We keep searching for solutions, standards, and rules that will restore integrity, ethics, and public trust and confidence in our corporations. But did that public trust and confidence ever exist? Or was it merely a passive public acceptance of a past system of corporate governance that was tolerated by a relatively small percentage of the population who owned stock but was wholly unsuited to serve the activist millions of Americans who believed in the system and soon learned that those who managed and governed the corporations in which they invested had little interest in earning the trust and confidence of their stockholders?

Contributing Factors

A brief look at the major factors that contributed to the deterioration of our system of corporate governance during those years may help in understanding what went wrong and what is needed to *create*—rather than *restore*—public trust and confidence in our leading corporations and governing boards. The fact is that a symbiotic relationship developed between self-serving recreant executives who worked their impulses for personal gain and see-no-evil, hear-no-evil, speak-no-evil directors who believed that "check-the-box" governance would protect and enhance shareholder value. Scandals occurred and fraud was allowed to thrive because too many of our publicly traded corporations were governed by corporate boards whose directors:

- lacked independence
- failed to discharge their stewardship responsibilities
- were not committed and properly prepared
- lacked the requisite knowledge about the corporation's industry, business, and financial affairs
- failed to coordinate and contribute to the preparation of meeting agendas and to arrange for thoughtful discussion of sensitive board matters and concerns
- did not meet in executive sessions without management to allow an open discussion and review of management's performance
- did not spend enough time at board meetings and committee meetings to properly discharge their duties and responsibilities
- never fully understood their duties and responsibilities as independent fiduciaries and did not appreciate that their overriding duty was to the stockholders
- were unaware of—or did not understand—the corporation's strategy and/or failed to monitor the execution of its strategy
- tolerated a major shift in the balance of corporate power to the CEO
- failed to confront or criticize management and were reluctant to disagree among themselves for fear of "rocking the boat"
- failed to critically review the CEO's as well as senior executives' performance
- failed to critically analyze management's plans and proposals
- approved huge increases in executive compensation, including bonus awards and stock option grants that were not tied to performance goals and objectives
- did not understand the corporation's financial statements or what parts of the business were profitable and why

- did not understand and did not question the corporation's revenue recognition policies
- adopted complex financial arrangements, including derivative transactions, which neither they nor the corporate executives understood
- served on too many boards and, therefore, did not have the time to properly fulfill their director obligations
- failed to create a corporate culture that demanded integrity and compliance with the highest ethical standards
- failed to create and maintain an atmosphere of excellence in the boardroom.

Legislative and Regulatory Corrective Action

So how did Corporate America, federal and state governments, and the stock exchanges and regulators respond to these failures? Congress adopted the Sarbanes-Oxley Act of 2002, a comprehensive, wide-ranging law that affects nearly every aspect of the corporate governance of publicly held U.S. corporations.

The New York Stock Exchange and Nasdaq adopted comprehensive new corporate governance rules.

New rules have been adopted which substantially change the way corporations disclose information to the stockholders and the public at large, and the SEC has adopted a requirement obligating CEOs and CFOs of public companies to swear on the dotted line—that is, to certify that their financial statements and reports are accurate and not misleading—exposing these executives to possible criminal charges if their numbers turn out to be bogus.

Many large and small corporations acted quickly to adopt new "best practices" and approve and implement revisions to their governance structures, policies, and programs.

Those who manage and oversee our corporations began to recognize that effective corporate governance requires independent, qualified, knowledgeable directors who understand that they occupy a position of trust that demands integrity and a clear and overriding commitment to serve the best interests of the stockholders.

The Sarbanes-Oxley Road Map

Much has been said recently about the new rules and regulations designed to reduce, if not eliminate, corporate fraud; create transparency; and give investors the opportunity and right to see the unexpurgated results of operations and the real financial condition of the corporations in which they have invested. The speed with which the new laws and regulations were enacted was breathtaking—and necessary. Despite the fact that many unanswered questions (and therefore unexpected risks) remain, these changes in the laws should serve as valuable tools in the hands of informed independent directors to restrain and eventually eliminate the type of corporate misbehavior that became routine and ravaged the savings and future hopes of not only experienced investors but also—and even more sadly—innocent workers who believed in the market and its integrity and bet their retirements on its continued success.

Critics have already commenced the attack on the regimen of laws, rules, and penalties created by Sarbanes-Oxley. They argue that rigid rules won't reform the corporate world and that history has proven that you cannot legislate morality or ethical behavior. We have statutes that make bank robbery a crime, but people still rob banks.

The critics are partly correct, but the true value of the laws and the accompanying regulations is not so much that they control the business and operations of America's corporations, but that they create a road map to guide those who govern our corporations in creating a corporate culture encouraging and rewarding integrity, trust, candor, honesty, fairness, and responsibility in the same way companies have historically rewarded entrepreneurship and creativity.

The person who needs to lead the effort to create and maintain a corporate environment in which this culture can thrive is the person who has the responsibility of setting the tone at the top: the corporation's CEO. The tone and culture of our business enterprises, as well as the standards, ethics, and values of Corporate America, are formulated and enforced at the top—by the CEO, who is assisted by senior executives and guided and monitored by the oversight of a board of informed, skeptical, and vigilant directors. Stockholders rarely attend stockholder meetings and often do not possess the knowledge required to make important corporate decisions. They elect and rely on directors to perform that responsibility. Stockholders have traditionally had little impact on a corporation's success, except for their right to vote for or against members of the board and for or against actions submitted to them by the board and management for their approval. However, the days of the passive, if not somnambulant, stockholder appear to be over as global competition has intensified and large stockholders, including institutional investors, foundations, unions, and pension plans, have begun to take a more active role in assuring that excellence prevails in the boardrooms of the corporations in which they own stock.

Duty of Care and Duty of Loyalty

It is the right, and obligation, of

every director to be informed and to

act deliberatively with the diligence

and competence of a reasonably

prudent person in a similar situation

under like circumstances.

T he directors select the CEO and members of senior management and fire them if they fail to perform, replacing them with executives whose interests, they hope, are aligned with the interests of the stockholders and who are knowledgeable, ethical, and understand their fiduciary duties of loyalty, care, and candor to their stockholders.

Loyalty, care, and candor. These words describe duties that ordinarily need no definition but have special meaning when applied to corporate governance. These duties arise out of the legal relationship established by most state corporate laws in America, which generally tend to follow Delaware law and provide that the business and affairs of a corporation are managed by or at the direction of a company's board of directors.

In practical terms, what do these duties entail? The corporation is managed by its CEO and senior executives. The directors' principal responsibility, apart from selecting the management team, is to oversee management. And how this oversight responsibility is discharged is generally determined by the corporate laws of the corporation's state of incorporation, guided by the duties of candor, loyalty, and care.

Candor. The duty of candor does not require elaborate discussion since that duty is implicit in both the duty of loyalty and the duty of care. This duty requires that the directors make sure the information that the corporation provides to its stockholders is materially complete and accurate.

Loyalty. The duty of loyalty requires a director to act in good faith and in a manner reasonably and honestly believed to be in the best interests of the corporation and its stockholders, while seeking to avoid any conflicting personal gain or economic interest. If a conflict exists, the conflicted director should recuse himself from any deliberation or decision on the matter of self-interest. If a conflicted director does not recuse himself or herself or abstain, the action of the board must satisfy the "entire fairness" test. The burden of proving that a decision is entirely fair is very heavy, similar to the burden of proving a negative. So the fundamental lesson for a director, is act in good faith, avoid conflicts, and abstain if you have any conflicting personal or economic interest.

Care. The duty of care requires that a director be informed. It is the right, and the obligation, of every director to be informed and, after acquiring the appropriate information, to act deliberatively with the diligence and competence of a reasonably prudent person in a similar position under like circumstances. Being informed is not a passive undertaking. If the CEO doesn't provide the information the director reasonably requires to make a decision, he or she must insist on obtaining the information; give it careful consideration; and, if necessary, seek the advice of outside advisors before acting.

A leading case in which directors were held personally liable for a breach of their duty of care is *Smith v. Van Gorkom*, a 1985 Delaware Supreme Court decision. In *Van Gorkom*, the court held that the directors were grossly negligent and therefore were personally liable when they approved a cash-merger proposal that provided the stockholders with a substantial premium over the then market price of their stock. The premium ranged from 39% to 62%, depending on the methodology employed in calculating the gain. The court found that the board's action was grossly negligent since the board was not sufficiently informed and therefore the so-called "business judgment rule" did not afford them protection from liability.

Briefly, the court found that:

- the directors did not adequately inform themselves as to the CEO's role in authorizing the "sale" of the corporation and in establishing the purchase price
- the directors were uninformed as to the intrinsic value of the corporation
- given these circumstances, the directors, at a minimum, were grossly negligent in approving the sale of the corporation upon two hours' consideration without notice, without reviewing the terms of the proposed merger agreement, and without the exigency of a crisis or emergency.

While the *Van Gorkom* decision turned on the facts before the court, it serves as a dramatic reminder that board decisions must be made on an informed and deliberative basis and that the process employed in reaching a decision is a critical factor in determining whether the directors have satisfied their duty of care.

Business Judgment Rule

Why is it so important for a director to properly discharge his or her duty of care? Because if the directors are properly informed, act honestly and in good faith, have no personal or financial interest, and believe the proposed action is in the best interests of the corporation and is attributable to a rational business purpose (collectively the key elements of the "business judgment rule"), a court of law will not substitute its judgment for that of the board. The business judgment rule provides a judicial presumption that each of the key elements has been satisfied and that the directors have satisfied their duties of care and loyalty in good faith. The judicial rationale for this position is that judges will not replace the board's judgment unless the contesting plaintiff (who has the burden of proof) can overcome the presumption and show bad faith, lack of due care, or the absence of a rational purpose. If this were not the case, it would be unlikely that responsible individuals, who don't relish being second-guessed, would agree to serve as directors.

While the business judgment rule has broad application to board actions, it does not uniformly apply to all board actions. For example, in the case of an unsolicited or hostile takeover offer, where the board's response must be proportionate to a reasonably perceived threat, a modified version of the business judgment rule may be applied. In that case, a board may not be required to accept an offer even though the offering price includes a premium over the current market price—except where the corporation has decided to sell control of the corporation. The board's decision to reject an offer and to remain independent is protected by the business judgment rule if the decision is made on an informed basis and in good faith.

The modified business judgment rule also applies to a board's decision to adopt defensive measures, such as a stockholders' rights plan, otherwise known as a "poison pill," where the decision can be supported as a response that is reasonably related to the threat of an offer at an inadequate price or a two-tier tendered offer. In other words, the response must be proportionate to a reasonably perceived threat. As the Delaware Supreme Court colorfully stated in its 1995 decision in *Unitrin, Inc. v. American General Corporation*, "When a corporation is not for sale, the board of directors is the metaphorical medieval corporate bastion and the protector of the corporation's stockholders"...and "if a board reasonably perceives that a threat is on the horizon, it has broad authority to respond with a panoply of individual or combined defensive precautions, e.g., staffing the barbican, raising the drawbridge and lowering the portcullis."

You will not be surprised to learn that many directors who understand the protections afforded by the duty of care and the business judgment rule remain fearful that their informed decisions may nevertheless be challenged in a court of law. They ask, "So what happens when I am sued despite the fact that I acted in good faith, on an informed basis, without any conflict of interest or personal interests, and with reasonable belief that the actions taken were in the best interests of the corporation? The board fees and benefits can never compensate me adequately for prolonged, expensive stockholder litigation."

Loss of Reputation and Embarrassment

While the director's concern and fear are not illusory, certain protections against personal monetary liability are built into the system, including:
- indemnification—statutory as well as contractual
- Directors & Officers insurance
- legislative limits on directors' liability, which permit corporations to include in their corporate charters provisions eliminating or limiting the personal liability of directors for monetary damages for breach of the director's duty of care (but not for breach of the duty of loyalty, acts or omissions not in good faith, knowing violation of law, and certain other exceptions).

Although directors may not be financially liable for their actions or inactions, they still have litigation risks for the following two reasons.

First, a director must consider the damaging effect on his or her reputation if the corporation improperly recognizes revenue, improperly records its expenses, or engages in fraudulent activity. The annual director's fees and stock options are hardly adequate to compensate a director for his or her loss of reputation and the accompanying embarrassment resulting from the corporation's unlawful activity.

Second, while D&O insurance and indemnification may be a part of the director's protection against monetary loss, what happens when the D&O insurance is exhausted or when the corporation becomes bankrupt? In those circumstances, even if the director successfully defends himself or herself, the legal costs of his or her defense, which in a complex legal matter can range from $200,000 to $500,000, could be devastating.

Several years ago, I met with a client, a very successful and wealthy executive, who was considering serving as a director of a high-tech corporation that had just completed a very successful public financing. In an effort to fully explore his risks, I cautioned him about the potential liabilities a director of a young public corporation might incur if the corporation were to engage in improper or fraudulent activity. He advised me that he had reviewed the corporation's indemnification obligations as well as the D&O insurance coverage and was satisfied that he would be protected, assuming he satisfied his fiduciary duty of care. He also added that the CEO was a longtime friend who was an honest and effective executive.

I told my client that he had asked all the right questions and apparently was comfortable with the answers and protection afforded by the corporation. But I also asked him whether he was aware of the risks of personal exposure if the corporation were rendered insolvent and the D&O insurance funds were depleted, explaining that even though his performance as a director may have been exemplary, he might be subjected to a demanding pretrial discovery process; a rigorous, time-consuming production of documents; and irritating, if not ugly, depositions, all of which would require the advice and assistance of his own lawyer, whose fees and expenses he would be obliged to pay. I also cautioned him about the possible public embarrassment and the potential tarnishing of his reputation that would be associated with a corporate fraud suit. He responded that I was being too cautious and, while he appreciated my advice, he felt the risks were minimal.

So, what happened? He joined the board, and two years later the corporation was investigated by the SEC for fraudulent revenue recognition. A class-action stockholder suit was commenced, and my client was subjected to regulatory interviews; tortuous plaintiff depositions; and countless hours of preparation with his attorneys, whose legal fees—approximately $300,000—he paid personally because the D&O insurance funds had, in the process, been exhausted and the corporation had declared bankruptcy. After the dreadful saga ended, he pronounced, "No more directorships for me."

I tell this story not to frighten potential directors or to discourage their board participation, but to make the point that an ethical, knowledgeable director who performs his fiduciary duty responsibly may nevertheless suffer financial loss, personal pain, and sleepless nights.

Role of the Board of Directors

Excellent companies stay

excellent by regularly

challenging themselves.

Having briefly outlined the role of corporate directors in terms of their legal responsibilities, let's explore what directors actually do and what they should do.

Why Serve as a Director?

Despite the fact that 2002 was marked by highly publicized corporate governance debacles and inexcusable derelictions by directors in the discharge of their fiduciary duties, most corporate directors are honest, well intentioned, decent men and women. They believe they are serving as directors to promote the best interests of their stockholders. Their motivations for serving as directors may range from the selfless desire to build value for their stockholders to the vain or ego-driven need to be a part of the corporate establishment and to sit side-by-side with the corporate elite. Between those two bookends, a director serves because the CEO may be a friend who needs a sympathetic ear on the board or because the director is seeking to supplement his or her income, increase his or her wealth through stock option awards, make new contacts in the business community, expand his or her knowledge of a particular business or corporation, associate with existing friends, or make new friends. Or it may simply be because he or she enjoys the challenge and intellectual stimulus of serving as a director and assisting executives in the performance of their responsibilities.

CEO-Dominated Process

Back in the pre-Enron era, most directors became members of the board because the CEO knew them or knew of them through a friend or business acquaintance or because they belonged to an elite group of "professional directors" who supplemented their retirement income by serving on multiple boards. Even in those corporations that had a nominating committee with the responsibility for identifying and recommending the election of new directors, the CEO customarily took the lead, participated in the committee's deliberations, recommended his or her preferred candidate, and persuaded the committee and the board that the candidate should be nominated—and he or she usually was. And in the absence of any scandal or challenge, the stockholders cast their proxies in favor of the nominee. As a result, the CEO, in a not-so-subtle manner, assembled a board that was unlikely to rock the boat and was expected to be loyal to the CEO and to preserve the "collegiality" of the members.

What did many of the boards look like before Enron and Sarbanes-Oxley? Obviously, some boards took great care in vetting their prospective members, selecting nominees who were familiar with the corporation's business and strategy, understood their fiduciary responsibilities, appreciated the need to provide independent advice, and had the desire and energy to perform their duties responsibly to further the best interests of the stockholders. But other boards were populated with directors who were principally adept at disguising their own ineptitude. Let me recall a few of these in support of this observation.

The Fast Reader. About a week before the board meeting, the CEO sent a thick FedEx package to each board member, which included the materials to be discussed at the board meeting, along with the CEO's proposed strategic plan for the coming fiscal year. The CEO requested that each director study the plan carefully and be prepared to discuss management's proposals and to recommend revisions, additions, or alternatives. At 9 o'clock on the morning of the board meeting, immediately prior to the CEO's convening of the meeting, the "Fast Reader" director asks the CEO's secretary for a letter opener and then proceeds to open the FedEx package for the first time. Talk about being totally unprepared!

The Endearing Friend. He is the CEO's sycophantic former college roommate who started two corporations over the past four years, both of which failed within their first 12 months. He has never been known to cross swords with the CEO at a meeting and has a 100% pro-CEO voting record.

The Sleeper. He attends meetings to catch up on his sleep. Obviously sleep-deprived, he begins to doze off within the first five minutes and awakens intermittently for a bio break. His sleep problem is also ubiquitous, as he has managed to induce two of his fellow directors to doze off at recent dinner meetings of the board.

The Rapper. He tends to dominate the board discussions and has a view, opinion, or comment with respect to each matter discussed at the meeting. Often sententious, but rarely laconic, when he runs out of comments, he still continues to dominate the discussion by asking questions that are usually either irrelevant or could have been avoided if he actually read the board materials before the meeting.

The Internet Traveler. Just prior to the start of the board meeting, she powers up her laptop and journeys through her e-mail, the latest stock quotes, *The New York Times* editorial page, and Amazon.com's latest book reviews. On occasion, she moves from her computer to her Blackberry and, mindful of her need to refrain from further disturbing the meeting and other directors' concentration, frequently leaves the meeting to take or make calls on her cell phone.

The Know-It-All. Imperious and implacable, he has the answer to every question and the solution to every problem, all of which was gained through his vast experience in a broad range of transactions, his connections with important people, and his success in defending himself in the seven lawsuits plus two SEC investigations brought against him over the past five years.

I trust that these exaggerated stereotypes are, or will soon be, artifacts of the past. They contribute little, if anything, to the work of the board and, in fact, impede the board in the discharge of its responsibilities. So what are the board's principal responsibilities and how should the board best perform them?

What Should Directors Do?

Oversight Responsibility. The business of the corporation is managed by its executive officers and senior management under the direction of the board. The board is responsible for overseeing management's efforts to enhance stockholder value. In that capacity, a director serves as monitor, counselor, protagonist, and critic. The board's principal oversight responsibilities include:

- selection, evaluation, and compensation of the CEO and senior executives
- replacement of the CEO and senior executives if and when appropriate and development and implementation of a management succession plan
- review and approval of management's strategic plan and business objectives

- review and approval of management's financial plans, commitments of significant corporate resources, and material transactions not in the ordinary course of business.

In addition, the board works with the CEO to set the tone at the top. Just as in our national and local governments; our schools and universities; and our professional organizations, hospitals, and philanthropic organizations, the tone and culture of our business enterprises and the standards, ethics, and values of Corporate America are formulated and enforced at the top—by the CEO, with the advice and assistance of the board of directors. Corporations must create and foster a culture in which the interests of the directors are aligned with those of the stockholders and the directors make informed judgments that benefit the stockholders. In short, this is a culture in which good corporate governance prevails and key corporate decisions and actions are tested against the paramount question: "How does this benefit the stockholders?"

In light of Sarbanes-Oxley, to ensure that the right tone is set at the top, directors of public corporations have the responsibility to:

- oversee the corporation's compliance with applicable laws and regulations
- adopt a code of conduct and ethical guidelines and oversee their implementation
- adopt and monitor corporate programs and policies that promote transparency and full disclosure
- ensure that membership of the board includes at least a majority of independent directors
- establish an audit committee of the board that is independent, diligent, and financially literate
- establish a compensation committee of the board that is independent, adopts fair compensation programs, and prohibits unauthorized loans and perquisites
- establish a nominating and governance committee of the board that ensures the recruitment and education of informed directors, avoids conflicts of interest, and promotes ethical and effective corporate governance
- ensure that management has created an insider-trading program, a monitoring program to assess the corporation's internal controls,

and a disclosure committee to ensure accurate, timely, and fair disclosure

- create and oversee implementation of self-assessment programs to evaluate the performance of the board as a whole and the directors individually.

In addition, particularly in light of the new requirements imposed by Sarbanes-Oxley, the directors must keep abreast of the new obligations imposed upon them through continuing education sessions and attention to new developments as they are reported in newspapers and business and financial publications.

Excellent companies stay excellent by regularly challenging themselves. In the performance of their oversight functions, directors must understand that their oversight responsibility means more than observing and commenting. It assumes a relationship in which the director serves as an informed and challenging advisor, a conscientious overseer, an insightful critic, and a fearless advocate—whose first question, when asked to consider a significant proposal by management, is, "How does this help the stockholders?"

In this era of expensive, protracted, and what some might describe as "take no prisoners" litigation, it is likely that many qualified, experienced individuals will refuse to serve as directors of publicly owned corporations for fear of being exposed to embarrassing, painful, and often costly stockholder lawsuits, derisive criticism, or attacks from stockholders who expect more from their directors. A common refrain these days, particularly in light of the sweeping breadth, explicitness, and ubiquity of Sarbanes-Oxley and the wide-ranging new rules and regulations promulgated by the NYSE and Nasdaq is, "Who in his right mind would want to serve as a director given the current hostile director environment?"

Board Composition and Best Practices. Several governance experts have asked whether the comprehensive legislation encompassed in Sarbanes-Oxley and the new rules being promulgated by the New York Stock Exchange and Nasdaq are necessary or an exercise in overkill. They contend that most boards have honest, well-intentioned directors who are motivated to enhance stockholder value and have adopted and apply generally accepted best practices, such as:

- the majority of the board is independent

- board members are honest, intelligent, experienced, serve on a number of boards, and are recognized for their prominence
- the directors have an equity interest in the corporation and therefore their interests are aligned with those of the stockholders
- the boards have established audit committees, compensation committees, and nominating and governance committees
- the corporations have adopted codes of conduct and ethical guidelines
- the boards customarily meet in executive session after each regular board meeting
- the boards have separated the roles of the chairman and CEO or, where those offices are combined, have created a new position, commonly referred to as "lead director" or "presiding director."

Many of the corporations that captured the "corporate fraud" headlines during the past two years had already adopted some or most of these as well as additional best practices, and yet they failed to establish and maintain the type of good corporate governance that enhances rather than destroys stockholder value.

The question, therefore, is whether the new laws and the new rules of the exchanges that seek to codify many of these best practices will make a difference or become so burdensome that even the most conscientious director will find them impossible to perform. An equally relevant question is whether the current intense focus on corporate governance is misplaced.

Do We Need Professional Directors? The answer is not to disregard the new rules or the existing practices, but to bolster them by creating a corporate governance culture in which independence, integrity, knowledge, and commitment are combined to enable directors to perform their oversight functions responsibly. But skeptics argue that the directors, who are at best part-time monitors and advisors, can never be as knowledgeable about the corporation as the full-time management team. Therefore, the skeptics say, these directors will never be in a position to provide fully informed oversight.

The skeptics do not, however, suggest that the oversight role of the board should be changed or abandoned. Instead, they argue for a change in the makeup of the board. They believe that board responsibilities and obligations have become so complex that only "professional" directors are capable of providing effective service. A director is "professional," they explain, if he or she makes his or her living serving as a director, has the requisite experience, fully understands the duties of a fiduciary, and engages in continuing education programs to keep abreast of changes in the laws and in corporate governance best practices.

I disagree with those who seek to professionalize boards. First, stockholders might be uncomfortable relying on outside directors who make their living serving as directors, believing, rightly or wrongly, that they may fail to act as independently as they should if their independence could lead to friction in the boardroom, conflicts with management, and a resulting call for their early retirement. In short, professional directors might be inclined to avoid conflict or disagreement in order to keep their jobs and director's fees. It is likely that this would be especially true of retired or unemployed executives and others for whom director's fees constitute a significant part of their income. Also, historically, professional directors have not always been welcomed by other board members for whom service on the board is a part-time activity, principally because some professional directors often exhibit a know-it-all condescension, if not arrogance, toward those nonprofessional directors, who are looked upon as "amateurs." Nonetheless, having one or two directors who qualify as "professionals" can add great value to the board because of their knowledge and experience, so a judicious blending of professional and nonprofessional directors is advisable.

FOUR

What Values and Qualities Should Directors Possess?

The board has no room for

insouciant directors who are not

committed or who believe

they can serve by being

passive observers.

Enthusiasm and Active Participation. Whether professional or not, there are certain important values and qualities that an effective director needs. It goes without saying that commitment, independence, experience, integrity, and the willingness to listen are at the top of most lists. The board has no room for insouciant directors who are not committed or who believe they can serve by being passive observers. Directors should be enthusiastic and excited about their service on the board. If they are, they will devote whatever time is required to ensure that they are fully prepared and know enough about the corporation's business to perform their duties assiduously and intelligently. They should also care deeply about the stockholders as well as their responsibility to help enhance stockholder interests, particularly when a decision is required that involves choices that may affect stockholder interests more favorably than management interests—and vice versa.

Business Know-How. Directors must also have business experience, acumen, and know-how, as well as a better-than-passing knowledge of how corporations conduct their businesses and what pitfalls to avoid.

Courage and Ability to Challenge. A board cannot be effective unless its members possess and exercise good judgment, are financially literate, are able and willing to assume responsibility, and have the courage to say no to management when it proposes actions or policies that subordinate the interests of the stockholders to the interests of management or otherwise serve to reduce rather than enhance stockholder value.

Complementary Skills and Experience. To properly discharge its oversight responsibility and intelligently challenge management, the board must include knowledgeable members with a wide range of backgrounds, experiences, and skills. Not every director needs the experience and skills that the entire board, as a group, requires to perform its oversight responsibility. One director may satisfy the SEC's definition of a "financial expert" and therefore assist those on the board who have great difficulty reading and understanding financial statements and income statements and whose brains have a sclerotic reaction when they attempt to understand such concepts as hedging transactions, the expensing of stock options, revenue recognition principles, and amortization calculations.

Not every director needs to be fully informed about the patents and technology that give the corporation's products advantages over its competitors' products, but every director must know what the corporation produces and markets and the services it provides, as well as how those products and services compare to those of its competitors. A director does not have to be a semiconductor expert to serve as a director of a corporation that sells and markets semiconductor devices, nor does he or she need a degree in microbiology to serve as a director of a biotechnology corporation.

However, the board should, if possible, be composed of directors who, as a group, have the experience and skills that are collectively required to make informed board decisions and provide effective board oversight. The composite skills of the board's members and the ability and willingness of individual board members to complement each other and to rely on each other's knowledge and expertise will produce an informed board of directors who are not afraid to disagree and who can intelligently assess management's performance and evaluate the corporation's strategic direction.

Preparation and Continuing Education. Notwithstanding their exemplary experience and qualifications, directors who do not come to board meetings fully prepared to discuss and act upon the meeting agenda should either resign voluntarily or be removed by their fellow members. In an era when bad corporate governance is under attack and directors are being sued for failing to perform their fiduciary duties, a director who comes to board meetings unprepared should be told that his or her presence is no longer required and be invited to leave.

Preparation is a combined effort of the directors and the corporation. Every new director should attend a comprehensive orientation session as well as periodic continuing education sessions that are designed to:
- relate important historic events in the life of the corporation
- describe the corporation's governance structure and the role and responsibilities of the board's committees
- describe the background, experience, unique skills, and responsibilities of the corporation's senior executives and managers
- introduce the directors to the corporation's senior executives
- familiarize the directors with the corporation's principal facilities and their responsibilities
- explain the corporation's financial statements, particularly such principal accounting issues as revenue recognition and the account-

ing treatment of matters unique to the corporation

- review the corporation's strategic plan and principal business objectives
- inform the directors of the corporation's culture, operations, and goals
- advise the directors of the need for, and the objectives of, the corporation's major programs, including its compliance program, insider trading program, SEC reporting programs and procedures, and governance and ethical programs and guidelines.

Each director must set aside the time required to prepare for each board and committee meeting, actively participate in the board's discussions, and provide useful advice to management. In short, each member needs to be an active, informed, and constructive participant.

Independence and Commitment. Director independence and commitment are the engines that drive good corporate governance. Independence means that:

- management will have the benefit of the board's unfettered, best judgment
- the board will assiduously make decisions on the basis of what is in the best interests of the stockholders
- the board will expect and demand that management will deal honestly with the directors and ethically in the conduct of the corporation's business
- the "don't rock the boat" attitude that historically permeated the "clubby" or conflicted board will be a relic of the past and will be replaced by an attitude that encourages and, in fact, demands free and open discussion and constructive disagreement.

There is a danger that the independence requirement may disqualify a highly desirable candidate from service on the board because of a "tainted" business relationship with the corporation. For example, the candidate may be an executive of a valued supplier or a customer of the corporation whose business experience in the industry could provide unique insights to the corporation and its other directors, but he or she cannot satisfy the "independence" standard because the business relationship between the two corporations crossed permissible financial relationship thresholds. Nonetheless, since the current rules require that only a majority of the directors be independent, the corporation could still add the director to the board so long as that director does not serve on board committees whose entire membership must be independent. In short, boards should not be afraid to include directors who are not strictly independent within the meaning of the applicable rules and regulations if those directors can bring needed unique skills or valued experience that other directors may not have.

Disagreement Is a Virtue, Not a Vice

The requisite willingness to challenge management comes from independence and an understanding of the role of a corporate fiduciary. Not surprisingly, most corporate executives encourage and welcome the exploration of alternatives, thoughtful discussion of management's recommendations, differences of opinion, evaluation and exchange of new ideas, and even constructive criticism. However, a director's constructive criticism or strong disagreement with management or other board members is not likely to be received positively or unemotionally if the dissenting director is believed by his or her fellow directors to be untrustworthy or self-serving. If trust and honesty permeate the boardroom, board challenges and criticism are perceived as positive expressions intended to benefit the corporation and its management. If directors are reluctant to disagree, or their disagreement is greeted with neglect or derision, the board soon becomes a vacuous receptacle of conformity. Moreover, disagreement by a director usually ignites a discussion among the directors and, as a result of the discussion, a change in what might otherwise have been an ill-advised, unanimous decision.

Disagreement and challenges are not always well received, whether they come from management or the board. Therefore, directors must be aware that the manner in which they deliver the challenge often determines how the challenge will be received and how effective it will be.

Most directors are reluctant to rebuke or reprimand the CEO or senior management openly at board meetings, fearful that they might be viewed as hostile scolds or as dissonant adversaries. On the occasions where I have witnessed what might be characterized as "basher" behavior, a palpable tension fills the boardroom, the comforting collegiality dissipates, and embarrassment and anger are evoked, particularly if all of this comes as a surprise or if there is no trust between the affected parties. The result often is an unfortunate, unintended confrontation as well as a time-consuming diversion. This does not mean that a director should not be skeptical or refrain from legitimate criticism or that he or she must put aside his or her concerns. However, there are cogent ways of communicating that are not denigrating but effectively convey dissatisfaction while at the same time providing helpful, constructive advice. You can be audacious without being insolent.

The best advice to the basher is don't refrain from criticizing the CEO if it is deserved and serves the best interests of the stockholders, but don't be captious or self-righteous, and consider delivering your criticism and disagreements privately, in a nonhostile manner. For example, directors who are unhappy with their CEO's performance or with the CEO's recommendations ought to consider channeling the criticism and advice through the board's lead or presiding director or, alternatively, meeting with the CEO privately, perhaps at dinner the night before the scheduled meeting. In that setting, the director and the CEO can discuss differences honestly and unemotionally, react to recommendations without rancor or embarrassment, and perhaps reach a consensus that can then be constructively presented at the board meeting.

If a pre-board meeting dinner cannot be arranged, a telephone call prior to the meeting may be adequate. Do not, however, seek to reconcile differences by an exchange of reproachful letters or memoranda since they usually evoke rancorous responses "for the record" and do not provide the type of constructive give-and-take that comes with a personal face-to-face meeting that can serve to clarify a position or ameliorate differences. Moreover, the written word may be construed as an offensive act by the recipient, not because of the content but because of the provocative style in which it is written or simply because it creates a record. So keep it simple, meet personally if possible, and if not, pick up the telephone: talk and listen. Listening is especially critical, keeping in mind the helpful aphorism that "you never learn anything new by listening to yourself talk." And always remember: You can disagree without being disagreeable.

Role of the CEO

The CEO should seek to create a

board meeting environment that

encourages skepticism and serious

discussion and enables board

members to disagree constructively.

Know Your Board

To obtain the highest value from their company's directors, CEOs must diligently seek to know each board member's background, experience, special skills, special areas of interest, strengths, weaknesses, likes, and dislikes. Based on this knowledge, a CEO can generally predict how the directors will react to management's proposals, thereby enabling him or her to anticipate and prepare for board questions and disagreements and, in so doing, prepare a more informed and effective case for management's proposals.

The CEO should also ensure that the directors have the opportunity to interact with senior management, who can be a reliable source of valuable information to the board. This interaction will help the directors accurately evaluate the performance and capabilities of the senior executives. This responsibility has become increasingly important as directors become more actively involved in oversight duties and as they fulfill the new responsibilities that have accompanied the recent shift in corporate power from the CEO to the directors. The directors should know whom the CEO considers to be his or her most valuable executives and employees and who among the senior management team might be his or her likely successor.

In addition, the CEO should seek to create a board meeting environment that encourages skepticism and serious discussion and enables board members to disagree constructively—or, in the words of Harvard Business School professor Walter J. Salmon, to create "constructive dissatisfaction."

CEOs who engage in obscurity are likely to have short tenures. CEOs and senior management must be prepared to be open and speak clearly and honestly to the directors. If the directors are aware of the challenges the executives face, they can and should be helpful.

Every board ought have to at least one director who is a trusted, wise advisor to the CEO and can respond quickly and impartially when the CEO needs help and wisdom, whether it involves his or her relationship with the board as a whole or with a particular board member or advice regarding the presentation of controversial matters to the board for action. This advisor should let the CEO know the he or she will be available when needed to listen and talk over a problem with the CEO and provide the CEO with his or her best judgment.

Setting the Tone and Corporate Culture

The cultures at Enron and its ilk placed a premium on earnings growth—however that growth could be obtained—and on highly risky, "creative" business arrangements and accounting practices. Little attention was placed on developing or imposing a system of checks and balances on an out-of-control engine that caused a mammoth train wreck. The ethical caution lights either didn't work or their warning flashes were not visible to the passengers whose peripheral vision was obscured by their intense focus on wealth and fame at any cost.

Where were the oversight, integrity, ethical guidelines, and supervision that would have prevented the chaos that ensued? Where was the culture that promoted creativity and success, but also demanded that they be achieved legally and ethically? Were there no moral compasses within any of these organizations that could have averted their collapse? Apparently not.

What these corporations lacked was a corporate culture that insists on integrity even at the risk of restraining entrepreneurship; an environment in which senior management is not afraid to disclose, discuss, or act on misconduct that comes to its attention; and a system of corporate governance that has no tolerance for deceit and greed. Who is responsible for setting the tone within the corporation that promotes and rewards integrity and establishes the corporation's values? That person is the CEO, assisted by the senior management team with active oversight from the directors. It is the CEO who must take the lead in making the board an active part of the decision-making process, encouraging skepticism and dissent, and emphasizing the paramount importance of honesty and fairness.

The CEO's Role in the Decision-Making Process

Inexperience, ignorance, or fear have historically driven many unsuccessful CEOs to keep their directors out of the decision-making process. Why?

They were reluctant to disclose early warnings or bad news, based on the mistaken belief that with time management could get back on track, meet revenue projections, or raise the funds needed to finance the corporation's business or complete the development of its new line of products.

They believed that disclosure to the board of bad news or the need for board help would ineluctably lead the board to believe that management was weak, lacked leadership, and needed to be replaced.

They expected that the board would not understand or could not make a difference, firm in their belief that only management could solve the problem—or that a solution would appear *deus ex machina*.

If this sounds implausible or you think I'm making this up to prove a point, let me make it clear that the reactions I have just described occur frequently and are most common among CEOs and senior executives who are insecure or have had limited experience with corporate boards.

I recall a board meeting several years ago, held by a well-financed start-up, high-tech corporation, which opened with a shocking announcement by the CFO that the corporation would run out of money within the next five business days. You can guess what followed. The CFO was fired on the spot, and the CEO was speechless as he listened to the directors' railings about his failure to give the board advanced warning of a rapidly approaching financial crisis.

Avoid Surprises

A CEO who wants to keep his or her job should never surprise the corporation's directors with bad news. Rather, he or she must keep the board apprised of potential future problems before they occur, seek help from the board to avert or ameliorate those problems when they occur, and make the board an integral part of the decision-making process. This not only makes good self-protective sense because it lets the CEO benefit from the board's experience and advice and avoid unpleasant surprises, but also because, if the decision later turns out to be wrong, the CEO can take some comfort in the fact that the mistake was not solely his or her mistake, but a mistake made by the entire board after a candid, informed discussion.

The responsibility for fully informing the directors does not rest solely with the CEO and senior management. The board also needs to be actively involved in making sure that the flow of information from management to the directors is timely, accurate, and enlightening. This means that the CEO and the management team must (i) prepare board agendas that are designed to inform and update the directors on the performance (including the failures) of the corporation and future business problems and risks, (ii) ensure that the reports of senior managers scheduled to make board presentations are relevant and timely, and (iii) encourage a thoughtful discussion by the directors of proposals submitted by management to the board for approval.

What Keeps the CEO Awake at Night?

CEOs who follow best practices supplement their board meeting materials with a short, two-to-three page CEO memorandum which summarizes the good and bad that occurred during the past quarter (or other relevant reporting period), reveals the problems and concerns that keep them awake at night and focuses on the important matters that will be presented for serious discussion with the board at the scheduled meeting.

All matters presented to the board do not deserve equal time or equal effort. The most productive meetings are those that are preceded by a memorandum from the CEO focusing on the key matters to be discussed at the meeting. This memo should close with the following admonition: "The meeting will be devoted to a thorough discussion of the following important matters, for which I need and will seek your input, critical analysis, advice, and recommendations," thereby invoking the following implicit warning: "So you better be prepared."

The beauty of this approach is that if the decision, after board deliberation, turns out to be wrong, it is not the CEO's fault, but the result of a bad decision reached jointly by the CEO and the board and arrived at after careful review and analysis. It also helps make directors believe that management wants and values their wisdom and advice. Doesn't that make sense? Why then would a CEO ever elect to fly solo when it is in the CEO's and the corporation's best interests to make the board a part of the decision-making process—particularly with respect to critical corporate decisions?

Board and Committee Meetings

Avoid information overload

and mind-numbing presentations.

Setting the Meeting Agendas

Most of the board's work is conducted at its regularly scheduled board and committee meetings. Accordingly, careful attention must be directed to the preparation of the agendas for the meetings and the development of the background and other materials submitted to the board for their pre-meeting review. If there is a nonexecutive chairman of the board or if the board has appointed a lead director or presiding director, that person should seek out the recommendations and input from other board members and work with the CEO to develop the meeting agendas. If the board does not have a lead or presiding director, the board should designate a director to perform this function. A similar procedure should be followed for producing committee agendas, with the committee chair, the CEO, and senior management collaborating to develop appropriate agendas.

The board and committee agendas should be accompanied by the reports, memoranda, plans, and other materials that are to be discussed at the meetings and should be delivered to the board and committees sufficiently in advance of the meetings to allow the members to adequately prepare for an informed discussion of the materials and of management's recommendations and proposals.

Risk of Information Overload

The board or committee packages prepared by management and delivered to board members before the meeting provide important historic data regarding the corporation's past and projected performance (including charts, graphs, memos, reports, recommendations, and analyses) to assist the directors in evaluating management's proposals and predictions and are necessary to enable the directors to make informed judgments. However, these materials are often assembled in multiple heavy, thick binders which, stacked together, can reach a height of six inches to a foot. How much of this mass of material is read before a meeting? I suspect that even the most conscientious director is put off by the sheer volume—not to mention the frequent irrelevance—of the pre-meeting paper directors are expected to read and comprehend. If you want directors to be prepared, avoid information overload and focus on content and relevance.

The best pre-meeting board materials contain the following:

- a thoughtful, well-prepared briefing memorandum from the CEO that reviews recent performance, and briefly describes and analyzes the matters to be presented at the meeting, including a discussion of the decisions the CEO is seeking from the directors. This should be accompanied by analyses, best- and worst-case scenarios, and risk factors
- a short—one- to two-page—memorandum from each of the management team members who will be presenting at the meeting, summarizing the principal elements of their presentations—written in plain English
- backup materials that the directors will be asked to refer to and discuss during the course of the meeting.

Aids to the Intellectually Challenged

I don't recall when or how it began, but PowerPoint presentations have become the universally accepted way to deliver lectures, speeches, reports, and proposals. It probably started with consultants and government bureaucrats who are quite adept at producing multicolored charts, graphs, talking points, and data-filled slides that are designed to capture the listeners' visual senses and enhance their retention capabilities. But, like most good ideas, the PowerPoint presentation has become an overused, soporific device that competes with the presenter for the audience's attention and has, through its overuse, lost much of its effectiveness. Instead of containing one or two pages of concise bullet points, presentations have grown to dozens of slides of heavy text that the presenter reads word-for-word as well as charts and graphs that are impossible to read or decipher. These mind-numbing presentations, which have been described by some critics as "aids to the intellectually challenged," have to go. They need to be replaced by animated, relevant, focused presentations that zero in on the issues that the directors need to know to effectively perform their oversight function and to assist management in achieving the objectives and strategies jointly established by the board and management.

Equally antithetical to productive board and committee meetings has been the parade of executives and managers who join the meetings to report on the activities of the business unit they manage. Why is this a problem? Shouldn't the directors have the opportunity to hear from the operating executives and managers and engage in dialogue with them about the performance of their business units? The answer, obviously, is "of course," but the problem, as in the case of PowerPoint presentations, is that the practice has become bloated, with too many needlessly long management presentations, leaving very little time for the board and the CEO to engage in thoughtful discussions about matters that actually require serious board input and corporate action.

It is up to the directors to complain to the CEO if they devote too much time to listening to long, sophistical presentations and not enough time to focusing on what keeps the CEO and CFO awake at night; carefully reviewing and acting on the reports of the audit committee, compensation committee, nominating and governance committee, and other key board committees; evaluating changes in the corporation's strategic objectives; considering acquisition opportunities; and discussing the CEO's and management's performance and business priorities. All of these are matters that require serious, timely discussion. They should not be squeezed into the last hour of the meeting or, even worse, be addressed while the directors are assembling their materials and making the frantic rush to catch the late afternoon return flight home.

Frequency of Board Meetings

How often should directors meet? The common legal response is, "as many times as may be required for the directors to properly discharge their fiduciary responsibilities." The board should meet at least quarterly to review the quarterly performance of the corporation. In the post-Enron era, many corporations have increased the number of regular scheduled meetings to six or eight per year, while the average time devoted to board matters of large corporations (including non-meeting attention to meeting preparation) by an independent director has grown to approximately 150 to 250 hours a year.

The length of the meeting will help determine how many regular meetings are held. Boards that hold two-day meetings may need only four or five regular meetings per year, while boards that meet from 9 a.m. to 3 p.m. once each quarter may need to add two or more meetings per year to get their business conducted. Additional special meetings are held as needed, particularly when it's important to consider corporate matters that need the directors' attention prior to the next regular board meeting. Of course, consideration by the directors of a possible acquisition, potential adverse litigation, management changes, and other major issues affecting the corporation will require more frequent meetings. Committee meetings should generally be scheduled to coincide with board meetings to minimize travel and allow the committees to report promptly to the board on their deliberations and proposals.

Telephonic meetings may be necessary for quick action or to consider a matter that needs to be resolved before the next regular meeting, while regular meetings are customarily convened at the corporation's facilities where face-to-face discussions can take place and reactions of the directors to the discussions can be more accurately discerned.

Executive Sessions

Many boards routinely hold executive sessions without management attendance immediately after the regularly scheduled board meeting adjourns. The purpose of the executive session is to give outside directors the opportunity to evaluate the proposals and plans recommended by management at the meeting and thereby allow each outside director to evaluate management's performance candidly. This practice is desirable because it encourages candor and provides the freedom to speak openly and avoid publicly embarrassing the CEO and other senior executives.

Experience has shown that holding the executive session after each board meeting, whether or not an executive session is really necessary, alleviates the anxiety and tension management may feel if the executive session were called for a specific purpose, leading the CEO to worry: "What did I do wrong?"

Whether the executive session is held regularly or only convened on an as-needed basis, it is important that the chairman of the executive session meet with the CEO promptly after the session is adjourned and inform him or her of the matters discussed and convey any suggestions or recommendations the session produced.

Board Compensation

The recent corporate scandals have affected both the demand for qualified, independent directors and the size and mix of director's fees. To attract experienced men and women who are willing to make a substantial commitment to board affairs and to subject themselves to the risks of costly stockholder litigation, corporations will need to pay their directors larger annual cash retainers, board and committee fees, and committee chairman retainers. They will also continue to award their directors with equity compensation, although the equity portion of their compensation may be reduced while the cash portion increases. Some corporations have decided to eliminate stock options for directors altogether. The reason for this change is the current belief that the huge stock option packages granted to executive officers and directors during the dot-com boom encouraged them to focus on short-term operating results rather than long-term performance, and, as a result, the interests of the executives and directors were not aligned with the interests of the stockholders.

Cash now appears to be the preferred payment alternative, but those corporations that still favor an equity component may impose stock-ownership requirements on their directors, which would obligate outside directors to acquire (either by grant from the corporation or by purchase) and retain a minimum number of shares over a specified period (e.g., three to five years). It is likely that an increasing number of U.S. corporations will adopt board stock-ownership guidelines.

According to a February 28, 2003, study by the compensation consulting firm Frederic W. Cook, Inc., based on an examination of the 2002 total compensation for boards of directors included in the Nasdaq 100 as of December 31, 2002 (companies with median revenues and market capitalizations of roughly $1.3 billion and $4.2 billion, respectively):

- average annual compensation for outside board members was approximately $250,000, of which about 90% represented the equity value of stock and stock option awards. The balance represented cash compensation paid for board and committee memberships and service as a committee chairman—assuming each board met six times a year and each committee met four times a year

- the compensation paid to board members in 2002 decreased by about 50% from its 2001 level, primarily because of the decline in the corporations' stock prices
- median annual retainers were approximately $20,000
- median board fees and committee meeting fees were $1,500 and $1,000, respectively
- median cash retainers per committee chairman were $4,000, and option grants were 5,700 shares
- annual present value of stock option grants ranged from approximately $85,000 at the 25th percentile to approximately $300,000 at the 75th percentile.

While it may be helpful as a benchmark for a corporation developing a director-compensation program to know what other corporations pay their directors, it is important to keep in mind that many factors will affect their ability to pay more or less than the surveyed corporations. These include the reputation and standing of the corporation; the attraction of service on its board; the revenue and profits of the corporation, and the resulting ability to pay directors compensation at or above the median amounts; and the peer benefits a director receives in serving on a board with members whose reputations and standing in the business world are widely acclaimed.

Most corporations have already taken action to significantly increase fees for members of the board's audit committee and compensation committee because the time that members of those committees must devote to comply with the new laws and regulations is expected to increase substantially. Directors will also receive so-called special duty pay for the special services they may be asked to perform, such as serving on litigation or investigating committees that the board establishes.

But boards must be ever mindful that stockholders and their lawyers may well contest special payments made to directors for the performance of their regular duties and responsibilities. It is unlikely that we will soon again see the type or size of payment that was made to a Tyco director— $20 million, which he shared with his favorite charity—for introducing a possible acquisition candidate to Tyco. After all, isn't that what a director is supposed to do?

Lead or Presiding Director

Historically, leaders of major U.S. corporations wore two hats, serving as both chairman of the board and chief executive officer. While stockholder activists have persuaded some corporations to split the position of chairman and CEO and to appoint a nonexecutive chairman in order to provide independent board leadership, it took the debacles of Enron and similarly misguided corporations to cause directors to accept the independent leader concept, a concept that is becoming more widely accepted as a board best practice.

Although some business executives reject the lead director concept because they believe it is likely to set off power struggles or lessen the CEO's authority, others believe it is a necessary reform that will aid in shifting control of the boardroom from the CEO to the board of directors.

Some CEOs are also fearful that assigning the chairman's title to an independent director creates a dangerous and confusing new level of authority. Their response typically has been, "You can't run a corporation with two leaders." Flexible boards have reacted to this fear by selecting a lead or presiding director or by adding the duties of a lead director to the duties and responsibilities of the chairman of the governance committee, with the authority to:

- assist the CEO in setting board agendas
- ensure that management provides directors with the information they need to do their job
- preside at executive sessions of nonmanagement members of the board
- make sure that the board's evaluation of the CEO's performance is properly conducted
- serve as a liaison between management and the board in times of crisis.

SEVEN

Committees of the Board

Excessive CEO compensation

is the "Mad-Cow Disease"

of American boardrooms.

Although the boards of directors of most U.S. corporations meet on average from four to six times a year, much of the work they do is performed by standing committees, principally the audit committee, the compensation committee, and the relatively new nominating and governance committee. In addition, special committees are often established to deal with specific problems or issues. For example, the litigation committee might monitor major litigation or the investigation committee might keep an eye on an investigation the board initiated.

Like board members, committee members must rely on information prepared for them by the corporation's management team or by outside consultants or advisors. It is unlikely that there will be perfect symmetry between the information made available to the board and the committee members, not because management is seeking to withhold information, but because members of the management team will, since they are full-time employees, be more informed than nonemployee directors who are part-time monitors and advisors. Therefore, directors who are committee members may from time to time seek additional information not only from management but also from outside consultants or advisors, as well as assistance in analyzing the information or developing committee-sponsored programs and policies.

The composition and responsibilities of the three standing committees must, in large part, conform to requirements set forth in Sarbanes-Oxley and by the exchange on which the corporation's stock is listed.

Audit Committee

The audit committee monitors the integrity of the corporation's financial statements, the independence and qualifications of the independent auditors, the performance of the corporation's internal and independent auditors, the corporation's compliance with legal and regulatory requirements, the effectiveness of the corporation's internal controls, and the nature and extent of any permitted nonaudit services provided to the corporation. The audit committee is also responsible for retaining, compensating, and evaluating the corporation's independent auditors, and, if appropriate, recommending their termination.

Sarbanes-Oxley requires that all members of the audit committee must be "super" independent, that is, they receive no payments other than director's fees, and they are not affiliated with the corporation. All members must be able to read and understand financial statements. At least one member ought to be a "financial expert," and the corporation will be required to disclose annually whether it has at least one "audit committee financial expert" on its audit committee and, if so, the name of the expert and whether the committee is independent of management. If the corporation does not have a financial expert, it must disclose that fact and explain why not.

The term "audit committee financial expert" was used in the final rules adopted by the SEC to emphasize that the designated person should have characteristics that are particularly relevant to the functions of the audit committee, such as:

- a thorough understanding of the audit committee's oversight role
- expertise in accounting matters, as well as an understanding of financial statements
- the ability to ask the right questions to determine whether the corporation's financial statements are complete and accurate.

The full board of directors must make the determination of whether an audit committee member qualifies as an audit committee financial expert. This term is defined in the SEC's final rules as a person with all of the following five attributes:

- an understanding of generally accepted accounting principles and financial statements
- the ability to assess the general application of such principles in connection with the accounting for estimates, accruals, and reserves
- experience preparing, auditing, analyzing, or evaluating financial statements that present a breadth and level of complexity of accounting issues that are generally comparable to the breadth and complexity of issues that can reasonably be expected to be raised by the corporation's financial statements, or experience actively supervising one or more persons engaged in such activities
- an understanding of internal controls and procedures for financial reporting
- an understanding of audit committee functions.

To qualify as an audit committee financial expert, a person must have acquired these attributes through any one or more of the following means:

- education and experience as a principal financial officer, principal accounting officer, controller, public accountant, or auditor, or experience in one or more positions that involve the performance of similar functions
- experience actively supervising a principal financial officer, principal accounting officer, controller, public accountant, auditor, or person performing similar functions
- experience overseeing or assessing the performance of corporations or public accountants with respect to the preparation, auditing, or evaluation of financial statements
- other relevant experience.

The audit committee must have the authority to engage independent counsel and other advisors it deems necessary to discharge its duties.

The final SEC rules include a safe harbor for persons determined to be audit committee financial experts. A director who is determined to be an audit committee financial expert will not be deemed an "expert" for any purpose, including, without limitation, for purposes of Section 11 of the Securities Act of 1933, as a result of such designation or identification. In addition, the safe harbor provides that the designation or identification of a person as an audit committee financial expert does not impose on the audit committee financial expert any duties, obligations, or liability that are greater than the duties, obligations, and liability otherwise imposed on such person as a member of the audit committee and board of directors. Such determination, however, does not affect the duties, obligations, or liability of any other member of the audit committee or board of directors.

The audit committee must adopt a committee charter that will describe the committee's duties and responsibilities. The charter should also be discussed with the corporation's independent auditors and be submitted to the full board for its approval.

The audit committee must perform its duties and responsibilities aggressively and intensively. A committee member who is passive or uninformed should be promptly replaced. The complexity of the committee's work and the importance of its position as the primary overseer of the tone at the top require that its members attend frequent meetings and dedicate long hours of preparation.

The guiding principle should be: "Trust, but verify." Committee members must bore into the financials, ask the difficult questions, say no for a transaction that cannot be properly explained, and have the courage to stand up to management and the auditors. The new certifications required of the CEO and CFO, while comforting, will not excuse an audit committee member from liability for his or her failure to effectively perform his or her oversight responsibility.

Members of an audit committee who meet a couple of times a year during a rushed one-hour breakfast meeting before a regularly scheduled board meeting are likely to find themselves as defendants in financial fraud claims brought on behalf of the corporation's stockholders. Given the complexity and importance of the audit committee's work, failure to meet at least four to six times a year (depending on the size of the corporation and the complexity of its business and financial statements) will increase the risk that a court of law will find that the committee did not properly discharge its responsibilities.

Each member should be aware of the corporation's critical accounting policies and should have up-to-date knowledge of significant new accounting and auditing announcements as well as new developments that affect financial reporting, including the following issues, which have been the focus of recent stockholder lawsuits:
- revenue recognition
- restructuring charges
- impairments of good will
- capitalized expenses
- bogus revenue
- derivative transactions
- swaps and barter transactions
- abusive use of reserves.

Also, remember that a corporation may experience a number of transactions, none of which is "material," but may be material in the aggregate. Therefore, each of these transactions should be questioned and understood to determine whether the "sum of all the immaterials" is material.

In connection with its implementation of Sarbanes-Oxley, the SEC adopted rules to direct national securities exchanges and national securities associations to condition the listing of any company on compliance with the Sarbanes-Oxley's audit committee requirements.

Compensation Committee

The compensation committee has the responsibility for reviewing and approving the corporation's compensation and benefits policies and objectives; determining whether the corporation's officers, directors, and employees are compensated according to those objectives; and discharging the board's duty to determine the compensation of the corporation's executives.

The New York Stock Exchange requires the establishment of a compensation committee, all members of which must be independent and must act independently of management. The committee must retain its own consultants and seek to compensate management in a reasonable, cost-effective manner.

The compensation committee must also adopt a charter, approved by the full board, that describes the committee's duties and responsibilities. The charter will be particularly helpful in eliminating any confusion or turf battles that might arise between the full board and the committee. In addition, the committee should establish principles governing the awarding of bonuses and incentive compensation, including determining whether bonuses should be tied to long-term performance in order to eliminate or mitigate the abuses that have resulted from a short-term focus on quarterly or annual operating results.

The Nasdaq rules governing executive compensation differ significantly from the NYSE rules. The directors are not required to establish a separate independent compensation committee, but executive compensation must be approved by either an independent compensation committee or a majority of the independent directors. If the full board is to make the final determination regarding executive compensation, after the CEO has presented his or her recommendations to the board all executives serving on the board (including the CEO) must recuse themselves from participating in the board's deliberations and decisions.

Because it has such a visible, direct effect on the corporation's profits, executive compensation has become one of the most prominent governance issues. Over the past several years, executive compensation surged, largely because of the hefty gains stock-based incentive plans provided. In the minds of many stockholders and regulators, the levels of cash compensation and bonuses paid to the executives of large U.S. corporations were excessive, if not outrageous, although some supporters might justifiably argue that the compensation of the leaders of America's largest corporations should be at least equal to or in excess of the lofty compensation levels enjoyed by this country's top professional athletes, movie stars, and investment bankers.

During the stock market boom and the irrationally exuberant, unprecedented climb in daily stock prices during the late 1990s, executive compensation skyrocketed, fueled principally by lavish stock option grants to corporate executives. J. Richard Finlay, chairman of Canada's Center for Corporate & Public Governance, characterized the excessive CEO compensation of that period as the "mad-cow disease of American boardrooms," which moved "from corporation to corporation, rendering directors incapable of applying common sense."

At the time, directors and compensation committees were apparently devoting substantially more time and effort to compensation matters than to ensuring that the corporation's financial statements and operating results were being properly reported. Huge stock option grants played a major role in enriching management. These options had several benefits: Until they were exercised, the recipients (unlike stockholders who purchased and owned their shares) had no money at risk; if the price of the corporation's stock dropped, the out-of-the-money options were replaced with new options exercisable at the then lower market price. Angry stockholders who suffered major losses as the market collapsed called for change and an end to the bounty being dispensed by boards and their compensation committees.

It was also a period when favorable, sizable loans to executive officers became common events, running up into the billions of dollars—think of WorldCom's Bernie Ebbers and Adephia's John Rigas. Did the directors who authorized these loans ever ask how multimillion dollar loans might benefit the stockholders?

Despite Sarbanes-Oxley and its reforms, compensation committees continue to be faced with a multitude of complex compensation issues. Equities no longer have the holding power they once had, in light of the relentless, dramatic declines in stock values since 2001; stockholders are fed up with large executive salaries and giant bonuses not tied to performance.

Compensation committees have typically relied on compensation consultants to advise them on the factors commonly used to develop compensation programs and incentives. This practice has led to the use of benchmarking, that is, comparisons with the wages of executives paid by competitors or other corporations included in the corporation's peer group. The benchmarking approach resulted in higher compensation levels for all executives, including increases to match competitors' then-excessive compensation levels.

In effect, the compensation of executives was not dependent on the performance of their corporations, but on the compensation being paid to the executives of other corporations. Following that logic, the compensation committee believed it was acting responsibly, for how, it asked, could a diligent committee justify paying its corporate executives less than the amount paid to executives in the peer group—regardless of whether the corporation met its performance objectives. In many cases the corporate executives argued—and the compensation committee agreed—the corporation had to pay executives above-average compensation to keep its best performers happy and to attract needed new talent, going beyond even the guidelines offered by peer group comparisons.

Some critics of previous excessive compensation awards also attribute the excesses to the compensation consultants management retained for independent advice. These critics have wondered out loud whether any of the hired compensation experts ever had the independence of mind, if not the audacity, to advise their corporate clients that their executives were being paid too much and that their salaries should therefore be reduced. It is highly unlikely that this unwelcome advice would have been provided to corporations that left the selection of the compensation consultants to the CEO or CFO.

Another lesson that compensation committees should keep in mind in developing their corporations' compensation principles is that the interests of holders of stock options are not fully aligned with those of stockholders. In fact, it is clear that many of the executives who held sizable stock options in America's largest corporations never actually had any money in the game. They customarily followed the exercise of their stock options with an immediate sale of the newly acquired shares, primarily to raise the funds required to pay the income tax on the gain realized at the time of the option exercise (where the gain is equal to the amount by which the value of the acquired shares at the time of exercise exceeded the option exercise price per share). Those executives who elected to retain the shares they acquired upon exercise of their options usually borrowed the funds needed to pay the tax on the gain. In hindsight, that proved to be astute if the value of the retained shares increased, but disastrous if the value of the retained shares declined.

In addition, it appears, contrary to past accounting policies, that the grant of stock options may soon be treated as a corporate expense at the time of the grant (if the accounting profession can agree on how to value the grants). Therefore, compensation committees will have an added incentive to develop equity-based programs for a corporation's senior executives, such as restricted stock awards, which avoid the stock option tax problems and the corporation's expensing problems while requiring the recipients to retain the stock they are awarded for a specified period of years, thereby creating the alignment with the interests of stockholders that was originally intended.

However, the tax treatment of restricted stock awards can be very burdensome, particularly if the recipient is prohibited from selling the stock for a specified period, and therefore action by the IRS may be needed if this form of equity compensation is to find favor among corporate executives.

While Sarbanes-Oxley has set the standards for the return of good corporate governance, comments made at a roundtable discussion on executive compensation in February 2003 by the chief justice of the Delaware Supreme Court indicate that Delaware courts might hold corporate directors legally liable if they do not act in good faith in approving executive compensation packages. The chief justice urged boards to "demonstrate their independence, hold executive sessions, and follow governance procedures sincerely and effectively, not only to guard against the intrusion of the federal government but [to] guard against anything that might happen to them in court from a properly presented complaint." He added, "If directors claim to be independent by saying, for example, that they base decisions on some performance measure and don't do so, or if they are disingenuous or dishonest about it...the courts in some circumstances could treat their behavior as a breach of the fiduciary duty of good faith."

This is an important warning, because, in the past, Delaware courts have been reluctant to review executive compensation packages, and now they have apparently expressed a concern about claims of independence relating to executive compensation.

Nominating and Governance Committee

Selection of Directors. The nominating and governance committee is charged with identifying qualified individuals to serve on the board of directors, recommending the director nominees to the board for the annual meeting of stockholders, and developing corporate governance principles and guidelines. The NYSE rules require that director nominations be approved by a nominating and governance committee composed solely of independent directors, while the Nasdaq rules require that nominations be approved either by an independent nominating committee or a majority of the independent directors. In addition, if the board conducts annual or other periodic evaluations of its performance and/or the performance of individual directors, this committee would be responsible for developing and conducting the self-evaluation process.

The committee needs to adopt an orderly process for the selection of director candidates, including:

- determining which talents, skills, and functional expertise are missing and conducting an orderly search for experienced candidates who can fill the gaps in core competencies
- selecting directors who are known to have good business judgment and are independent and unafraid to challenge conventional wisdom
- establishing reliable processes for conducting due diligence on director prospects and assuring that no invitation is extended to a prospect unless the committee so votes and authorizes one of its members to extend the invitation, ensuring diversity in the boardroom.

Some large stockholders, including institutional investors, pension funds, and unions, have urged that at least one member of the board of directors be nominated by stockholders; others have urged that two candidates be nominated for each directorship up for election, allowing the stockholders to select between the nominees. While the annual meeting proxy statements from U.S. corporations include an invitation to stockholders to submit recommendations for board membership, these invitations have, until recently, produced few serious stockholder responses. But this lassitude has been diminishing, and a growing, well-organized movement is developing among stockholder activists seeking to require the nominating and governance committee to change the process and allow at least one of the stockholders' designees to be nominated to the board. To facilitate the process, some stockholder groups are seeking to maintain a pool of professionally qualified independent director candidates. The resistance to this requirement stems largely from the belief that each of the independent directors selected by a nominating and governance committee represents the interests of the stockholders and is not beholden to any special constituency; therefore, structuring the process to guarantee a specific slot for a "stockholder designated nominee" is unnecessary, disruptive, and improperly casts doubt on the independence of the nominees selected by the nominating and governance committee.

Code of Business Conduct and Ethics

Sarbanes-Oxley requires each public company to disclose in its reports whether or not (and if not, why not) it has adopted a code of ethics for its senior financial officers. The NYSE, however, requires each listed company to adopt and make publicly available a code of business conduct and ethics for the company's directors and all its employees, and corporate governance guidelines addressing matters specified in listing standards. Nasdaq requires each listed company to adopt a code of conduct addressing, at a minimum, conflicts of interest and compliance with applicable laws and regulations; a compliance mechanism; and disclosure of any waivers to executive officers and directors.

The code of conduct is intended to deter wrongdoing and promote the conduct of the corporation's business in accordance with high standards of integrity and in compliance with all applicable laws and regulations. These include:

- honest and ethical conduct, including the ethical handling of actual or apparent conflicts of interest between personal and professional relationships
- full, fair, accurate, timely, and understandable disclosure in reports and documents that a corporation files with, or submits to, the SEC and in other public communications the corporation makes
- avoidance of conflicts of interests, including voluntary disclosure of any potential relationship or transaction that might give rise to such a conflict

- compliance with applicable governmental laws, rules, and regulations
- the prompt internal reporting of code violations to an appropriate person or persons identified in the code
- accountability for adherence to the code.

Corporate Governance Guidelines

The corporate governance guidelines are intended to guide the board as it exercises its governance duties and responsibilities. They should include:

- a listing of director responsibilities
- establishment of effective systems
- director qualification standards, including independence, size of the board, limit on other directorships, tenure, retirement, duties of lead director (if appointed), and selection of new director candidates
- board meeting processes and procedures, including selection of agenda items; frequency and length of meetings; advance distribution of materials; executive sessions; board committees' membership and charters; director access to management and independent advisors; director compensation (and form of compensation); director orientation and continuing education; management evaluation and succession; annual performance evaluation of the board; and board interaction with institutional investors, the press, and customers.

While new laws and regulations may serve as a road map for the creation of public trust and confidence in a corporation's accounting and disclosure systems and compensation practices, something more is needed to create public trust in executive leadership. What is needed is a proactive CEO who believes in corporate integrity and ethical behavior; who acts ethically; who talks explicitly and repeatedly within the corporation of the need to promote integrity; who denounces overreaching; and who makes believers of the corporation's officers, employees, customers, suppliers, and advisors. His or her message must resonate throughout the corporation and instill all employees with the resolve to help create a corporate culture that nourishes integrity and ethical behavior, flowing from both the top down and the bottom up and penetrating all aspects of the corporation's business and governance.

Qualified Legal Compliance Committee and the "Noisy Withdrawal" Quandary

On January 23, 2003, the SEC adopted final rules to implement Section 307 of Sarbanes-Oxley by setting "standards of professional conduct for attorneys appearing and practicing before the commission in any way in the representation of issuers." In addition, the SEC approved an extension of the comment period on the "noisy withdrawal" provisions of the original proposed rule and publication for comment of an alternative proposal. The rules adopted by the SEC will, among other things:

- require an attorney to report evidence of a material violation, determined according to an objective standard, "up-the-ladder" within the corporation to the chief legal officer (CLO) or the chief executive officer of the corporation or the equivalent
- require an attorney, if the CLO or the CEO of the corporation does not respond appropriately to the evidence, to report the evidence to the audit committee, another committee of independent directors, or the full board of directors
- clarify that the rules cover attorneys who provide legal services to a corporation with which they have an attorney-client relationship and who have notice that documents they are preparing or assisting in preparing will be filed with or submitted to the SEC
- allow a corporation to establish a qualified legal compliance committee (QLCC) as an alternative procedure for reporting evidence of a material violation. The QLCC would consist of at least one member of the corporation's audit committee, or an equivalent committee of independent directors, and two or more independent board members. It would have the responsibility, among other things, to recommend that a corporation implement an appropriate response to evidence of a material violation. An attorney can satisfy the rule's reporting obligation by reporting evidence of a material violation to a QLCC
- allow (but not obligate) an attorney, without the consent of the corporation, to reveal confidential information related to his or her representation to the extent the attorney reasonably believes it neces-

sary to prevent the corporation from committing a material violation likely to cause substantial injury to the financial interests or property of the corporation or investors; prevent the corporation from committing an illegal act; or rectify the consequences of a material violation or illegal act in which the attorney's services have been used.

In addition, the final rules establish an objective, rather than a subjective, triggering standard, involving credible evidence based upon which it would be unreasonable, under the circumstances, for a prudent and competent attorney not to conclude that it is reasonably likely that a material violation has occurred, is ongoing, or is about to occur.

As proposed, the rule would impose a duty on outside counsel to effect a noisy withdrawal as counsel if the corporation fails to respond within a reasonable period of time to reported violations or if it fails to respond appropriately. The noisy withdrawal obligation would require counsel to give prompt notice to the SEC of its withdrawal, indicating that the withdrawal was based on professional considerations and promptly disaffirming any opinion, document, affirmation, characterization, or the like in (or incorporated in) a document filed with or submitted to the SEC that counsel has prepared or assisted in preparing and that counsel reasonably believes is or may be materially false or misleading.

It was no surprise that leading securities practitioners objected to the noisy withdrawal provision on several grounds, in particular that its application would constitute a damaging encroachment on the attorney-client relationship. While I am unable to predict how the SEC will resolve the issue (although I expect a compromise will be the result), the new rules—with the mandatory up-the-ladder reporting scheme and the statutory protection of whistle-blowers—will significantly enhance the ability of the board of directors to perform their critical oversight responsibility and create a corporate environment that is free of dishonesty, fraud, and illegal activity.

EIGHT

Revolt of the Stockholders

2003 will be remembered as the

year when stockholder activists

took steps to change the way

their corporations are governed,

their directors are nominated, and

their executives are compensated.

In his February 21, 2003, annual letter to the stockholders of Berkshire Hathaway Inc., Warren E. Buffett, chairman of Berkshire's board, made the case for greater involvement by large stockholders in reforming corporate governance. He wrote:

"When the manager cares deeply and the directors don't, what's needed is a powerful countervailing force—and that's the missing element in today's corporate governance. Getting rid of mediocre CEOs and eliminating overreaching by the able ones requires action by big owners. The logistics aren't that tough: The ownership of stock has grown increasingly concentrated in recent decades, and today it would be easy for institutional managers to exert their will on problem situations. Twenty—or even fewer—of the largest institutions, acting together, could effectively reform corporate governance at a given company, simply by withholding their votes for directors who were tolerating odious behavior. In my view, this kind of concerted action is the only way that corporate stewardship can be meaningfully improved."

Rule 14a-8 under the Securities Exchange Act of 1934 generally requires a corporation to include proposals submitted by stockholders in the corporation's proxy statement for presentation to a vote at a stockholders meeting. This rule permits an owner of a relatively small number of the corporation's shares to present a proposal to the stockholders unless the corporation can convince the SEC to issue a letter stating that it will not recommend enforcement action against the corporation if it excludes the proposal from the proxy material because it falls within one of the 13 provisions of the rule that permit exclusion or does not satisfy the rule's procedural requirements. The most commonly used exclusion has been the "ordinary business exception." This allows the corporation to exclude a stockholder proposal if the staff of the SEC determines it relates to the corporation's ordinary business.

Advocates of greater stockholder involvement have significantly increased their participation in the annual meeting proxy process over the last several years. During the first quarter of 2003, stockholder advocacy groups filed a record number of stockholder resolutions for inclusion in the annual meeting proxy statements of many of America's largest publicly traded corporations. The number of stockholder proposals in 2003 will far exceed the record number submitted in 2002. As a result of both the increasing popularity and use of stockholder proposals and the movement to eliminate the ordinary business exception, the SEC has agreed to undertake a comprehensive review of its proxy rules regarding stockholder proposals.

The stockholder-proposed resolution route has traditionally been used primarily by stockholders advocating social and environmental reforms. In the aftermath of Enron, however, this practice has become increasingly popular among those stockholders who are advocating changes in corporate governance designed to make America's publicly traded corporations more trustworthy and stockholder-oriented.

The Issues

The proposals encompass a number of important *corporate governance issues*, including:

- pay disparity and excessive CEO compensation
- the separation of the CEO and chairman positions
- elimination of classified boards
- stockholder approval of poison pills
- expensing of stock options
- tying executive pay to performance
- performance-based indexed stock options
- executive severance arrangements
- director-election processes, including stockholder nominations for board positions
- board diversity
- mandatory binding effect of majority stockholder vote.

The leading *social issues* encompassed by the proposals include:
- the environment, including climate change and measurement of greenhouse gases
- health care and health issues
- global labor standards
- drug development
- human rights

- equal employment opportunities
- the global AIDS crisis.

Historically, angry stockholders voted with their feet. If they didn't trust corporate management or disapproved of the corporation's performance, they would sell their shares and invest the proceeds in corporations whose management and directors reacted positively to stockholder concerns about corporate governance issues and social issues. Now these stockholders are angry and prepared to fight, rather than walk away. Their battle cry is, "We are owners of the company and we no longer intend to walk away from the battle, but are determined to fight for what we believe."

Although stockholder resolutions are not binding (even when they do receive a majority vote), they nevertheless put public pressure on the corporation's management and board and constitute a public expression of anger or dissatisfaction. This can embarrass management and eventually lead to less resistance by management and the board—and even acquiescence.

While the movement toward increased stockholder participation may be healthy and timely, many boards caution that it would be a mistake to mandate that stockholder proposals that receive a majority vote should bind the corporation. They submit that independent directors are presumed to have the ability and knowledge to determine whether implementation of a stockholder-approved proposal, although meritorious, would be harmful or inimical to the corporation's operation; could adversely affect segments of the corporation's business; or would, on balance, be detrimental to its relationships with its employees, customers, or suppliers.

These boards further contend that if the directors don't have the requisite knowledge or experience or if they fail or refuse to listen to the stockholders, the remedy is not to turn over the governance of the corporation to thousands of stockholders. Instead, they suggest, the boards should function as every representative form of government does—with stockholders submitting their own nominees for election to the board and voting for directors who more accurately reflect the views of the stockholders or who, if they disagree with the stockholders, are able to demonstrate that their disagreement is based on their independent and informed judgment of what is in the best interests of the corporation and its stockholders. They might also find comfort in the words of Thomas Jefferson, who warned, "You should not undertake great departures on marginal majorities."

Despite strong resistance by this country's mutual funds, the SEC decided in early 2003 to require all publicly traded mutual funds to disclose annually how they voted the shares of stock of corporations they own on matters submitted by the corporations for action by their stockholders at annual stockholders meetings. This disclosure will, for the first time, allow stockholder advocacy groups to determine how the funds voted. This is information that will be especially helpful to stockholder advocacy groups in planning strategies intended to secure favorable fund votes for their proposals and negative votes on matters presented by the board and management that they oppose. While the availability of the funds' voting records may lead to increased pressure and lobbying by stockholder activists aimed at convincing the funds—particularly those with substantial stock ownership—to vote with them, no assurance can be given that the funds, which have their own agendas and areas of interest, will be persuaded to do so by the stockholder activists. Nonetheless, the new voting disclosure requirements will certainly create important opportunities through which battle-trained stockholder advocacy groups can influence the votes of some of the largest owners of stock in America. This, in turn, may increase the power and influence of stockholder advocacy groups and enhance their opportunities to win proxy fights that they have historically lost.

This new SEC reporting requirement is also in line with statements made by SEC commissioner Cynthia A. Glassman, who, on March 12, 2003, warned that "regulations can only go so far"; they "cannot legislate ethical behavior." She noted the important role of insiders and "gatekeepers" (including stockholders; inside management; and outside parties such as auditors, attorneys, and audit committee members) in preventing breakdowns in corporate governance, while adding, "Active and informed investors act as another check on corporate management.... The notion of an educated shareholder as a good corporate citizen dovetails with good investor education."

While confrontation is often necessary, stockholders who seek changes in corporate governance or a corporation's position on social or economic issues should first consider a positive educational approach. If that doesn't work, they should consider the stockholder-proposal confrontational approach. Providing the management and board with a thoughtful and balanced position paper setting forth the benefits of the action proposed by the stockholders—and following this with an in-person information session with management, during which the proponents can present their position, answer management's questions, and focus on the merits of the proposal—may lead to agreement between the stockholders and management and obviate the need for a confrontational, public proxy battle. Moreover, education can be a two-way street; management may be able to persuade the stockholder proponents to drop their proposal or defer it.

CalPERS, the country's largest public pension fund, maintains a "Focus List," which identifies companies CalPERS believes should follow better corporate governance practices. Companies that are added to the Focus List are generally subject to widespread criticism, which can be embarrassing to the named companies and generate anger from their stockholders. Once a company is included in the Focus List, CalPERS requests a meeting to discuss how the company intends to address CalPERS' concerns about the company's corporate governance. If the company refuses to meet or to make the changes, CalPERS attempts to apply pressure through stockholder proposals or proxy campaigns.

The year 2003 will be remembered as the year when bold action was initiated by stockholder advocates seeking to change the way their corporations are governed, their directors are nominated, their executives are compensated, and their defenses against unsolicited takeovers are approved. The success of their advocacy will depend on their ability to persuade directors that the proposals they advocate are reasonable, are important to the corporation, require immediate action by the stockholders, and are designed to enhance shareholder value and instill stockholder confidence and trust in the governance of the corporation. The risk is that multiple stockholder-sponsored proposals may be confusing and perceived as overkill and may dilute or turn off otherwise favorable stockholder reactions while generating fervent opposition from management and the board because of their number, complexity, and lack of relevancy. Focus, persuasion, and open communication, including coordination among advocacy groups with different agendas, are therefore critical to the corporation's support of the proposals and ultimately to stockholder approval.

Scorekeepers

During the opening months of 2003 there was a noticeable increase in the influence of the "scorekeepers" who analyze, judge, and rate the corporate governance and accountability practices of publicly held corporations. Institutional Shareholder Services (ISS), which was founded in 1985 and advises many institutional investors during the annual proxy period, has created the "Corporate Governance Quotient" (CGC) to rate corporations on eight major topics and more than 60 subsets of issues, including board structure and composition, charter and bylaw provisions, executive and director compensation, supermajority voting requirements, director independence, directors' and officers' stock ownership, and director education. These scores are available to subscribers—including large stockholders, mutual funds, and pension plans—and influence the corporate governance reputations of the scored corporations. A corporation that scores poorly risks being viewed negatively by institutional and other large investors, which, in turn, may use the low scores to bolster support for their proposals.

Other scorekeepers who influence corporations that they rate include Domini 400 Social Index, TIAA-CREF, CalPERS, the AFL-CIO Office of Investment, and the Council on Institutional Investors. The Investor Responsibility Research Center announced in 2003 that it would join forces to develop a corporate governance rating system based heavily on quantitative factors. The influence of these organizations on the corporate governance and social responsibility of the corporations they evaluate has increased substantially, both as a result of their efforts to make U.S. corporations more responsible to their stockholders and the communities in which they reside and as a reaction to the corporate excesses and abuses that have provoked broader stockholder activism as well as new legislative and regulatory initiatives designed to create public trust in critical elements of our corporate world and economic system.

However, scorekeepers that rate corporations on 50 or 60 issues may be less effective than if they rated them on 10 or 15 of the major issues that determine good corporate governance. Too much data diminishes the value of the data, and the most important findings are often lost in the shuffle.

In addition, a corporation may be very profitable, highly ethical, and resolute in abiding by the most conservative financial accounting and reporting rules and yet be ranked below less successful corporations as a result of the low scores it receives because all of its directors are not independent, or its directors failed to attend prescribed corporate governance continuing education programs during the past year, or one or more directors have passed the scorekeeper's mandated retirement age. Therefore, while the published ratings may provide useful information, investors should be judicious in how they are applied and measured.

Evaluation of Board Performance

Self-assessment of directors'

performance is receiving

increasingly wide acceptance

as board members realize that

they are in the best position to

evaluate their board performance.

ost corporate governance guidelines require an annual self-evaluation of the board's performance, as well as an assessment of its policies and objectives. Self-evaluation, which has been receiving increasingly wide acceptance, is based on the belief that the directors themselves are in the best position to evaluate their performance.

While assessment of the performance of the board as a whole has not been a controversial practice, peer evaluation—or assessment of the individual performance of each director—has not been generally favored, primarily because directors don't want to be put in a position of criticizing their colleagues. Nevertheless, assessment of individual director performance is gaining acceptance as fiduciaries struggle in the post-Enron era to gain the trust and confidence of stockholders.

The value and acceptability of board assessment are dependent, in large part, on the process used in conducting the assessment. Most boards are likely to assign the assessment function to the nominating and governance committee, which, having the responsibility for selecting and nominating director candidates, should also have a thorough knowledge of how well the board is performing and which board talents and expertise are needed for improved board performance.

In the assessment of individual board member performance, each director should be asked to evaluate his or her co-directors'
- independence
- commitment
- contributions
- willingness to challenge management
- competencies
- personal characteristics
- ability to function as part of a team.

The assessment criteria should (i) correspond, in large part, to the criteria established for the nomination of directors; (ii) be linked to the principal duties and responsibilities that the board is expected to perform; and (iii) be benchmarked against the board's agreed-upon goals and objectives for the relevant assessment period. The assessment will only prove to be beneficial to the directors—as well as to management and stockholders—if the process encourages directors to perform the difficult task of critiquing the performance of their colleagues individually and as a group. This requires honesty, fairness, courage, and a good dose of diplomacy.

At the beginning of each year, the board should prepare and prioritize a list of its objectives and goals for the year. Shortly after the end of the year, the board should review how it has performed, using its stated objectives as benchmarks against which its performance will be measured. The review should include a thoughtful discussion and analysis by the directors at a board meeting scheduled for this purpose, as well as a compilation of responses the directors made to a board-performance survey or open-ended questionnaire.

Organizations that focus on corporate governance issues and the education of corporate directors have developed extensive checklists and guides for assessing board and individual director performance, some of which may also be used to conduct or assist in the evaluation process.

The following are some of the more important questions that, if properly answered, would help in evaluating both the board's and the individual director's performance.

Evaluation of the Board

- Are the directors independent, enthusiastic, and fully committed to serving on the board?
- Do the directors have business savvy and the requisite knowledge about the corporation's business and competition?
- Do the directors have the desired mix of skills and expertise the board as a group requires?
- Are the directors prepared for board meetings?
- Has the board determined its duties and responsibilities and the expectations of each director?
- Has the board identified and prioritized those issues it believes should be discussed with management on a regular basis?
- Is the board willing to challenge management when required—to fire a manager who is mediocre?
- Does the board review, approve, and monitor the strategic plan developed by management?
- Does the board have an up-to-date, corporatewide succession plan in place?

- Does the board regularly evaluate the performance of the CEO and other senior executives?
- Has the board adopted a management compensation plan that fairly and effectively rewards performance?
- Have the directors and the CEO created a relationship that promotes open and frank discussion?
- Have the board and its committees been productive and effective?
- Does the board work well with the CEO and other executives?
- Are the directors properly and fairly compensated for their services?

Evaluation of Individual Directors

- Is the director committed?
- Does the director attend all scheduled board and committee meetings?
- Is the director prepared for the meetings and in a position to make informed decisions?
- Does the director understand his or her fiduciary duties and legal obligations?
- Is the director available to the CEO for consultation or advice when needed?
- Is the director objective, or does he or she tend to "rubber-stamp" management?
- Is the director too passive, indifferent, or unwilling to challenge management?
- Does the director contribute positively—with constructive criticism, creative solutions, and positive recommendations?
- Does the director have good judgment?
- Does the director have inestimable value, special skills, unique knowledge, or special relationships or contacts that are helpful both to other directors and to management?
- Does the director interfere with management—that is, does he or she seek to manage the corporation rather than oversee its management?
- Is the director obdurate, acerbic?
- Is the director aware of the corporation's compliance programs and procedures, including its ethical code of conduct? Has the director made an effort to ensure that they are implemented and observed?

Effect of Sarbanes-Oxley on Private Corporations

Good corporate governance is

good for business, whether the

business is large, small, public,

private, or even nonprofit.

While Sarbanes-Oxley will dramatically change the way publicly held corporations behave by mandating specific, comprehensive corporate governance rules and guidelines, it generally has no legal application to privately held corporations. However, that does not mean that the governance systems and best practices that publicly held corporations are adopting in response to the new federal law will be ignored by privately held corporations.

The fact that a corporation is not publicly owned does not excuse it from conducting its affairs openly and ethically, nor does it mean that the corporation will not benefit from developing a more effective system of corporate governance. In the post-Enron era there will be increasing pressure on privately held corporations, nonprofit institutions, and universities and colleges to adopt some of the reforms and new governance structures and practices that their public counterparts have already adopted, because they are confronted daily with many of the problems that public corporations ordinarily face. In addition, the owners of private corporations and the trustees of nonprofit institutions are likely to conclude that the new rules and best practices make good business sense and will benefit and enhance the value of their entities. If the new rules restore honesty, fairness, and ethical behavior to public corporations, they are likely to become objective standards by which both public and private corporations and nonprofits will be judged.

Given the exposure of Sarbanes-Oxley, trustees and directors of nonprofit institutions, particularly those that receive funds from private donations or government grants or contracts, would be well advised to consider changes in their codes of conduct, more intensive review of compensation packages, and greater care in reviewing the affiliations (and independence) of members of their audit committees. Directors or trustees of these institutions have the responsibility to oversee management and are bound by fiduciary duties of loyalty and care and therefore have fiduciary obligations to ensure that the institutions operate honestly and ethically. Moreover, many corporate directors of public corporations serve on the boards of nonprofit entities, and it's likely they will require the management of those entities to adopt some of the governance best practices that evolve as a result of the changes mandated by Sarbanes-Oxley. Also, many nonprofit institutions that receive federal funds are required by the Federal Office of Management and Budget to perform an annual audit mandating an assessment of the entity's internal controls over financial reporting and the specific programs receiving federal funds—although this assessment is not as comprehensive as that required of public corporations by Sarbanes-Oxley.

Except for small, family-owned businesses, which have their own unique benefits and problems, most private corporations have a long-term strategic exit or liquidity strategy. In the case of venture-financed corporations, the venture investors typically plan to take the corporation public, merge with a public corporation that has an active market for its stock, or sell the corporation or its assets for cash or freely tradable securities. The public investors or potential purchasers of the corporation will expect that the corporation has operated its business honestly and ethically.

Moreover, a private corporation that is about to launch an IPO will be able to perform more comfortably in the public arena if it has a prior history of operating as if it were a public corporation—that is, if its board has experience with independent directors; the directors serving on its audit committee are financially literate; it has adopted, observes, and enforces a code of ethics; and its executive compensation system is fair and will withstand careful public scrutiny. When the prospectus is written for the IPO, the corporation's historical governance structure and practices will be closely scrutinized. If they portray a disciplined corporation that has followed generally accepted governance best practices, investors are more likely to view the corporation favorably and have greater confidence in its management and directors.

Even if the corporation never goes public, the trickle-down effect of Sarbanes-Oxley will change the way many small, private corporations manage their affairs, because private corporations that are ethical and have good corporate governance and independent directors are more likely to attract and retain loyal employees, customers, and suppliers. In short, good corporate governance is also good for business, whether the business is large or small, public, private, or nonprofit.

Model Board

The model board's membership

includes individuals with diverse

talents, experiences, personalities,

instincts, and expertise that provide

the composite skills that produce

excellence in the boardroom.

A t the risk of embarrassing myself, but emboldened by a better understanding of how and why so many prominent, large U.S. corporations, beginning with Enron, succumbed to management fraud, scandalous behavior, and board neglect, I have developed my own version of the ideal or model board of directors of a publicly owned U.S. corporation.

My model is based in large part on my experience with boards of several hundred corporations founded during the 30-year period commencing in the early 1970s, which were funded by a then relatively small group of experienced venture capital firms or private investors. Those corporations were generally founded by senior or midlevel executives, engineers, scientists, or entrepreneurs who had spent several years in responsible operating, engineering, and marketing positions at large U.S. corporations, such as IBM, General Electric, and Xerox. The founders had little, if any, experience managing a corporation or dealing with corporate boards or stockholders. Most of the venture investors did have substantial board experience, having served on the boards of the corporations they helped finance.

Partners of the principal venture firms that financed the new enterprises customarily served as directors of those enterprises and worked closely with management to:

- add experienced directors to the board, who possess skills and expertise the board needed or desired
- find and employ key members of the management team, such as the chief financial officer, vice president of sales and marketing, and vice president of research and development
- provide guidance and advice to management in the development and monitoring of the corporation's strategic plan
- help develop compensation and benefits plans for executives and employees
- raise additional equity funds for the corporation when needed
- provide experienced and wise counsel and judgment
- develop programs and policies to ensure ethical behavior, accurate accounting, and compliance with governmental rules and regulations.

These directors were also usually:

- knowledgeable, committed, and actively involved
- independent of management

- willing and able to disagree and to challenge management
- aligned, as major stockholders, with the interests of the corporation's stockholders
- unafraid to fire the CEO and other senior executives if their performance should warrant termination and to locate and recruit their successors
- motivated to make the corporation successful as soon as possible.

In the '70s and '80s, venture capital investors (VCs) were long-term investors and understood that it would take seven to 10 years before they could expect to trigger a liquidity event that would allow them to profit from their investment, either by creating a public market for the corporation's stock or by merger with another corporation or a sale of its business and assets. However, beginning in the late 1990s and continuing through the initial years of this century, the VC's investment goals changed substantially. This was particularly true during the period the dot-com lunacy prevailed and infant one- or two-year-old corporations, with no earnings and only the prospect of significant revenues, were able to consummate initial offerings of their stock to the public at mind-boggling valuations or were acquired by corporations like Cisco and Lucent at prodigious valuations that had no relationship to either historic revenues or earnings, which usually were nonexistent. As a result, the long-term investment objective of the average venture capitalist shifted from seven to 10 years to two to three years. In many cases it dropped below two years.

The earlier the liquidity event, the sooner the VC could distribute the appreciated stock to its fund investors and distribute its shares to its VC partners. Also, once they distributed the shares, most venture capitalists resigned their board seats since they had only a small stake or even no stake in the corporation. This allowed them to devote more of their available time to the corporations in which they continued to own stock or to new corporations they intended to fund. This short-term focus, coupled with a growing misdirected tendency of certain venture investors to seek to manage the corporation rather than provide oversight to its management, helped make the venture investor a less attractive candidate for the model board, despite the fact that he or she had many of the qualities and attributes of a highly desirable board member.

The search for an ideal board member is a feckless exercise. The ideal board does not require a board of like-minded, like-qualified directors. What's necessary is a combination of individuals with diverse talents, experiences, interests, instincts, and expertise that together provide the composite skills that produce excellence in the boardroom.

While a board's composition and needs will vary depending on the company's business, size, location, financial performance, and competition, the exemplary board of a publicly traded U.S. corporation should be made up of directors who contribute complementary expertise and skills and possess at least the following qualities, traits, and characteristics.

Directors

A majority of the members of the board must be independent (as defined by the regulations of the exchange on which the corporation is listed), and each director should:

- be enthusiastic about serving on the board and be prepared to provide that service in a timely and constructive manner
- have business know-how and experience
- have a real interest in the business conducted by the corporation
- be focused on enhancing stockholder value
- understand and faithfully discharge his or her fiduciary duty of loyalty and duty of care
- be committed to remain fully informed about the corporation's business, products, industry, and competition
- have the ability and the will to say no, to rock the boat, and to disagree with and challenge management, while carefully refraining from assuming management's role
- possess integrity and commitment to high ethical standards
- possess sufficient knowledge and experience with accounting and financial matters so as to qualify as being financially literate
- understand and diligently discharge the responsibility for selecting; compensating; and, when necessary, terminating the CEO and senior executives and selecting their successors
- possess sound business and strategic judgment and the ability to oversee and monitor management's development and implementation of the corporation's strategic plan

- be capable of developing and evaluating fair compensation and incentive and benefit plans for the executives and employees
- understand the need for—and require management to provide—prompt, fair, and full disclosure of material events affecting the corporation
- be willing and able to function as part of a team
- be willing to resign and depart the board—noisily if appropriate—in the event the CEO and management refuse or are unable or unwilling to create and maintain a corporate culture that demands integrity and ethical behavior at every level of the corporation's workforce
- be committed to asking the right questions and evaluating management proposals, always guided by the need to answer the paramount question: "How does this benefit the stockholders?"

The Board

The board, as the governing body of the corporation, should:
- be large enough and include enough independent directors to allow it to staff the three principal board committees (audit, compensation, and governance) and, unless independent directors are expected to serve on more than one committee, optimally include between seven and nine independent directors
- ensure that a majority of the members of the board are independent
- be composed of individuals who possess the complementary expertise and skills the board requires
- select one of its members to serve as the lead or presiding director to coordinate the board and committee agendas and actions with the CEO of the corporation, serve as a link between the board members and the CEO, and preside at executive sessions of nonemployee members of the board
- schedule six to eight regular, full-day board meetings annually
- schedule at least four regular meetings of the corporation's principal board committees (except for the audit committee, which should meet more frequently)
- schedule committee meetings the day or evening before the regular

board meetings to permit unrushed, thoughtful discussions

- advise each board member to expect to commit 150 to 250 hours (or more for larger or more complex entities) annually to the performance of board and committee responsibilities
- pay its directors fairly for their services, including their time spent at board and committee meetings; for their services as committee chairs; and for their time devoted to special assignments and preparation for board, committee, and management meetings
- require that the audit, compensation, and nominating and governance committees each adopt a written charter defining its duties and responsibilities and be led by a chairman with expertise and/or experience in the matters for which the committee is responsible
- adopt guidelines that limit a director's participation on other boards unless otherwise expressly permitted by the board
- ensure that the board's membership includes directors who have CEO, executive, or senior management experience; knowledge of the industry in which the corporation competes; and experience in developing and/or monitoring strategic plans, executive compensation programs, and evaluation of senior executive performance
- work with management to ensure that the corporation has developed an appropriate corporate strategy and monitor management's execution of that strategy
- conduct periodic evaluations of the performance of the board as a whole, as well as the performance of each board committee and each board member individually
- ensure that the corporation has adopted appropriate compliance programs, a corporate code of conduct, corporate governance and ethics guidelines, and corporate disclosure policies—and is committed to their enforcement and to prompt and fair disclosure
- adopt a director-compensation plan that provides fair and appropriate compensation (both cash and equity) for each nonemployee director
- ensure that, if it does not have a formal retirement policy or a limit on the number of years a director may serve, the board adopts and implements a policy of periodically adding new directors to provide fresh ideas and missing-but-needed skills and experience, and to replace directors whose performance becomes marginal or inadequate.

The Essence of Excellence

Experts may differ on what is needed to instill public trust and confidence in America's major corporations and financial markets. Evaluating a corporation's board to determine whether it merits being rated "excellent" requires both objective and subjective assessments. The objective assessment is easier to accomplish because it involves comparing what the directors do to what they should do. If the "should do" checklist properly describes the board's duties and responsibilities, the resulting rating should provide a relatively accurate, objective evaluation of the board.

The subjective assessment, however, is more daunting because it encompasses an evaluation of important human attributes, including experience, attitudes, personality, ethical values, diplomatic skills, communication skills, courage, honesty, toughness, fairness, and the ability to set the right tone.

Therefore, even if the board as an entity and the directors individually are conscientious, committed, and well-intentioned, excellence will be absent in the boardroom unless the directors:

- trust and respect each other
- are fully committed to serving the best interests of the stockholders rather than their own or management's best interests
- are willing to challenge management and fellow directors and to be challenged in an environment that welcomes constructive skepticism as well as free and open differences of opinion
- are able to set a tone at the top that censures extravagance, greed, dishonesty, fraud, self-dealing, deception, and disloyalty and extols integrity, ethical behavior, and decency
- successfully establish a corporate environment that embraces, embodies, and nurtures a culture that rewards those who deserve to be rewarded and dismisses those who deserve to be dismissed
- insist that both management and the board, prior to acting on an important proposal or recommendation, answer the transcendent question, "How will this enhance stockholder value?"

While no board is or will be perfect, a board whose members possess and are guided by these skills, qualities, attitudes, and values has the ability, power, and incentive to intervene; shape the corporation's direction;

and, through the process of acculturation, create a corporate environment in which excellence will flourish and endure not only in the boardroom but throughout the entire corporation and ethics and integrity will be at the core of every decision.

About the Author

Paul Brountas joined Hale and Dorr in 1960, became a senior partner in 1968, and was appointed senior counsel to the firm in 2003. At Hale and Dorr, he has served as chair of the Corporate Department, the Executive Committee, and the firm's Strategic Planning Task Force.

While his practice has encompassed most areas of corporate and securities laws, he has focused on the representation of start-up and emerging growth companies; venture capitalists; issuers, investors, and underwriters in public and private financings; companies, stockholders, and investment bankers in mergers and acquisitions; and corporate directors, both as counsel to corporate boards and as outside counsel to independent directors.

Brountas has earned a reputation as one of the nation's leading high-technology lawyers. The *National Law Journal* selected him as one of the "100 Most Influential Lawyers in America," *Boston* magazine named him one of "Boston's 100 Most Powerful People;" and *Electronic Business* magazine named him one of the top 10 high-technology lawyers in the United States. He is also listed in *The Best Lawyers in America* and in *Chambers USA America's Leading Lawyers*. His clients have looked to him not only for legal advice, but also for his judgment as a business counselor and problem solver.

Brountas has been a frequent lecturer and speaker at various professional and trade association programs, ranging from venture capital financings, joint ventures, and public offerings to mergers and acquisitions, corporate governance, and duties and responsibilities of directors. For several years, he also served as a guest presenter at Harvard Business School's entrepreneurial management course. He is the author of "Counseling the

Public Company," published as part of *Massachusetts Business Lawyering* by Massachusetts Continuing Legal Education, Inc.

In 1987 and 1988, Brountas served as national chairman of the Committee to Elect Michael S. Dukakis President of the United States.

He served as chairman of the board of trustees and president of the board of overseers of Bowdoin College.

Brountas received his law degree from Harvard Law School and his undergraduate degree from Bowdoin College. In 1954, he was awarded a Marshall Scholarship for study at Oxford University, where he received both B.A. and M.A. degrees from the Oxford Honors School of Jurisprudence.

Brountas lives with his wife, Lynn, in Weston, Massachusetts. They have three children, Paul Jr., Jennifer, and Barrett.